GARY LIBRARY

WITHDRAWN VERMONT COLLEGE

MONTPELIER, VT.

Please remember that this is a library book,
and that it belongs only temporarily to each
person who uses it. Be considerate. Do
not write in this, or any, library book.

WITHDRAWN

We Take This Child

WITHDRAWN

WITHDRAWN

CLAIRE BERMAN

We Take This Child

A Candid Look at Modern Adoption

DOUBLEDAY & COMPANY, INC.   GARDEN CITY, NEW YORK
1974

ISBN: 0-385-02476-2
Library of Congress Catalog Card Number 73-9142
Copyright © 1974 by Claire G. Berman
All Rights Reserved
Printed in the United States of America
First Edition

Excerpts from "The Adoption of Mentally Retarded Children" by Ursula M. Gallagher, January–February 1968 issue of *Children* (now *Children Today*).

Excerpts from ADOPTING OLDER CHILDREN by Alfred Kadushin. Copyright © 1970 by Columbia University Press. Reprinted by permission of the publisher.

Excerpts from "Furor Over Whites Adopting Blacks," by-line Judy Klemesrud, April 12, 1973 issue of New York *Times*. Copyright © 1973 by The New York Times Company. Reprinted by permission.

362.734
B516w

For Reva
And in loving memory of Max—
My parents.

In a special way for Steven, who started it all.

30226

30226

Acknowledgments

For their time and knowledge, I would like to thank the following persons: Mae Neely, director of New York City's Department of Adoption Service; Barbara Lewis, former executive director of the Adoption Resource Exchange of North America; Gwen Davis, the able and informed librarian of the Child Welfare League of America; Kathryn Donley, executive director of Michigan's Spaulding for Children, for going beyond education to friendship; Sydney Duncan, executive director of Detroit's Homes for Black Children and her most co-operative staff; Ruth Carlton, women's metro editor of the Detroit *News;* and Clayton Hagen, former supervisor of adoptions for Minnesota's Lutheran Social Services, for enlightenment.

Among the many members of citizens groups who spoke with me, directed me, and sent their excellent newsletters to keep me up to date, I am especially grateful to: Eve Smith, formerly executive director of New York's Council on Adoptable Children; Joyce Forsythe of Michigan COAC; and Flora Cunha of the Organization of Foster Parents for Equality and Reform.

For allowing me to share in their stories, both joyous

and painful, and for their insights born of experience, I want to thank innumerable adoptive parents and adopted children and adults, and yet I cannot name them here. They know who they are. Without their co-operation, there could not have been this book.

Contents

We Take This Child

Introduction

Todd will be six years old this summer. Born out of wedlock, he spent the first two years of his life in one foster home, is presently living in another. He is an even-featured, attractive, and bright child who had never had a health problem more serious than a cold and roseola—until recently, when he developed an eye ailment. It is feared Todd may lose the sight of one eye. In adoption circles, Todd is classified a "waiting child," subdivision: hard to place. Because he is older, and black, and male, and because he may be handicapped.

What Todd is waiting for is a permanent home and family. The director of the large adoption agency to which Todd has been referred is actively seeking an adoptive home for this outgoing young boy. Therein lies the most important feature of the new face of adoption.

Just a few years ago, there would have been no chance for Todd. Prospective adoptive parents who inquired at established agencies were almost exclusively white infertile couples who sought the standard adoptable child: an infant Caucasian, preferably female, who came complete with guarantee of perfection. If defects were later discovered, the child could be returned for exchange. Agencies, including the one with which Todd is listed, were set up to assist these couples, matching prospective adoptive parents with newborn adoptable babies: blue-eyed infants for blue-eyed adults. A child born out of wedlock to Betty Coed was earmarked for a professional couple with impressive IQs. Religious and racial lines were not crossed. (Only the family doctor would be able to tell the "real" family from the ersatz.)

But then society itself began to undergo great changes, which affected the makeup of "real" families. The high divorce rate plus the rising cost of living were societal factors leading to the acceptance of the small family. Ecological concerns and the movement to Population Zero took it one step further: the small family was not only acceptable, it was desirable. Couples who wished to rear large families were encouraged to adopt existent children rather than add more than two biologic children to this overcrowded planet. In some cases, the couple that decided to remain childless was not only accepted, but applauded. Nor was it difficult for such men and women to achieve their goal. Improved methods of birth control made it possible for persons to have as few children as they wanted. This had a great effect on the supply of babies born out of wedlock—very simply, it dramatically reduced the number of such births.

Where birth control methods either had failed or not been employed, new and liberalized abortion laws were effective in keeping down the total number of births. Over-all, there had developed a generally relaxed moral climate in which greater numbers of unwed mothers were able to keep and raise their children.

All of this has had its impact on the institution of adoption. Approximately six thousand fewer children were adopted in the United States during 1971 than in the preceding year, the National Center for Social Statistics reported, marking the first time since 1957 (when the Center began to issue annual reports on adoption) that the number of adoptions did not increase. When I told Arnold Lislow, director of New York's Talbot Perkins Agency, that I was writing a book on current trends in adoption, his forthright reaction was, "Why? There practically is no adoption." Mr. Lislow overstressed the situation, but the import of his statement is clear: there is little adoption as we all knew it once upon a time. Given the current situation, some adoption establishments are becoming multi-service agencies, employing their staffs and resources to develop new programs which stress pre- and postnatal counseling for the unwed mother and resident care for both mother and child. Under such programs, it is reasoned, mothers will be better able to make the difficult decisions concerning their own fate and that of their children. Those who elect to keep their babies will be aided in implementing that decision.

Other agencies, faced with dwindling files of picture-book babies, have been made to take a look at the children who *are* available and they've discovered the hard-to-place child: the black baby; the youngster of mixed race; the boy or girl who may have to go through life with a physical or mental problem; the child who has left infancy long behind him. They are also learning that people in our society are happy to become parents to these children. Thus, "hard to place" is constantly being redefined. Today, there are waiting lists for healthy infants of *any* color. The category of "older child" now is seen as "older and older." Families have come forward to express a readiness to cope with problems ranging from cross eyes and heart murmurs to cerebral palsy and mental retardation. In the past, such disabilities immediately made youngsters seem unadoptable to caseworkers, with the result that the judgment became the fact. The children in question were "unadopted."

Would-be parents have been made to decide: can we

accept and love someone other than a baby in mint condition or will we take a chance on not getting any baby?
This remains today's question, one which must be answered by each person who seeks to adopt.

Those who've said "yes" make up most of the matter
of this book. While no two stories of adoption are the
same, I've found common threads woven throughout the
experiences of those who've made similar adoption: the
white couple that adopts across racial lines; the family
that is tested by the older child it invites to become one
of its own; the man or woman who adopts, knowing that
years—perhaps a lifetime—of medical care for the child
are to be expected; the family that applies for a homeless
youngster from a distant land and an alien culture. Count-
less such families have shared their experiences with me
so that, through this book, they can speak to all persons
interested in adopting and say, "This is what you might
expect" and, to their fellow adoptive parents, "These experiences—which seem unique to your situation—have
been lived through by others. Perhaps it will be helpful
to see how we came through." In one chapter, a man and
wife who returned a child they had planned to adopt
speak with difficulty of the factors which led to their still-
painful conclusion. To those who make their living in the
work of adoption and whose decisions (or indecisions)
affect so many lives, the families are saying, "These have
been our satisfactions with the system and these our grievances. We hope you learn from them." Most of all, those
who welcomed me into their homes and their lives did so
because they believe in adoption. They know there are
children, today, waiting for homes. They hope to publicize
this fact. And so do I.

While the stories in this book are based on fact, the
histories presented are composites of innumerable interviews with adoptive families. Any resemblance—by name
or location—to actual persons is unintended. This has been

done out of respect for the confidential nature of the interviews and to protect the youngsters' privacy as we to give as complete a picture of each situation as c___ only be obtained by stepping away from the separate experiences for an overview of the greater reality. On the other hand, the professionals who've been quoted by name and affiliation are the actual persons interviewed. It is important to know who they are and where they stand and to appreciate their judgments against their backgrounds of experience and position. That many directors of agencies, caseworkers, volunteer workers, lawyers, and doctors took time from their work to talk of adoption is an encouraging sign of a new openness on the part of the adoption establishment, a willingness to inform but also to be questioned. There were some agencies that did not open their doors, whose representatives either put me off on one pretext or another or simply refused to speak "to the press," as they put it. Happily, they stand out as exceptions against a rule of candor.

Just as the definition of the adoptable child has broadened, so has the prescription for the perfect adoptive parent been reformulated. The stereotype used to be a couple just beyond their early thirties who'd tried to have a child of their own and failed. Proof of infertility often was required by the agencies to which they applied for an infant to adopt. The ideal adoptive couple had been married more than five years, and enjoyed a good relationship with each other and with members of their extended family. They belonged to the same church. There were no atheists who sat before the social worker. (Interestingly, the New Jersey Supreme Court recently upheld the right of atheists to adopt a child, setting a national precedent.) They enjoyed a good standard of living. Their finances were carefully investigated. The wife had to state that her greatest desire was to stay at home and care for a child.

There is a growing awareness that couples need not fit this picture to qualify as good parents. Many social agencies no longer set rigid age limitations for applicants. Young men and women in their twenties are applying for babies, often a decision they made prior to their marriage, while older partners deemed ineligible under past requirements are being allowed to adopt older children. There is certainly a growing tendency to relax the rules on income. In addition to promoting subsidized adoption, forward-looking workers assure applicants they care more about an impressive salary picture. Employment is now seen as acceptable for women, too. If a female applicant confesses her plan to continue working after she becomes a mother, this decision need not act as a barrier to adoption—just as long as she can show intelligent plans for the day care of the child.

Certainly the single parent, a dramatic innovation in adoption placement, must continue to work. Nevertheless, men and women in this situation are today being allowed to parent children. In a nation in which one out of three marriages ends in divorce, in which many children are being raised by one parent, it comes as no surprise to learn that single-parent adoptions can be successful.

Finally, a word about the children. Much is being said today about adoption becoming a child-centered institution, one which seeks to find a good home for a waiting child rather than, as in the past, the perfect child for hopeful, would-be parents. While this is increasingly true and just, the adoptive story does not end with placement, for the child of adoption grows to be the adult who was adopted when a child. Many of these grown persons live a continuing story of a search for identity and a battle for legal rights. It was not easy for some of these men and women to speak out; that they did—and do—deserves the attention of all who claim a serious interest in adoption today.

The Classic Tale —
to the Agency for a Healthy, White Baby

The classic adoption story has to do with two married partners, in their late twenties or early thirties, who were wed after she graduated from school (he may still have been in graduate study). Following a respectable period as newlyweds, they decided it was time to build a family. When a year went by, or longer, and the woman failed to conceive an heir, the couple's next step was to visit their family doctor. If inoperable medical problems were diagnosed, the physician most likely would have recommended the couple look into adoption. What's more, neighbors and relatives told of so many cases in which —how can it be explained?—couples conceived immediately after they'd adopted a child.

Whether motivated by this hope or accepting of the fact that biologic parenthood wasn't in their future, the husband and wife visited an adoption agency and began the process resulting in the placement of a beautiful, healthy infant in their home: a family was made. Was it just happenstance that the average period between application and placement frequently ran nine months?

Victoria and Owen Matthews, who fit neatly into the above story, know they were lucky to be looking for a

baby when there were babies to be had. Vicki, a
dancer, and Owen, now an executive with a small record
company but then doing walk-on roles in TV soap operas,
were into the fourth year of a childless marriage when
a gynecologic examination of Vicki revealed a tubal clos-
ing as the cause of apparent infertility. Motherhood,
while not out of the question, was considered unlikely.
"A 10 per cent chance" is how the doctor stated it for
the Matthews. A visit to a renowned fertility clinic con-
firmed the diagnosis.

Vicki didn't hesitate to look into the next possibility:
adopt a child. Owen concedes he was hesitant, that the
idea didn't come easily to him. He believes this, too, was
typical; many husbands have been moved to adoption by
their wives, for whom it has traditionally been important
to have children. (This is changing as more women find
career-oriented lives acceptable, even satisfying.) Owen
wondered, with a good deal of hesitation, what it would
be like to raise another person's child and mentioned,
only once, that perhaps they ought to wait a while. The
situation wasn't hopeless. There was that 10 per cent
chance to cling to.

Vicki expressed herself as against any plan that would
prolong the tension of that infertile period. "You don't
know what it's like each month," she said during our interview, time not dimming the memories of that difficult
period, "when you find out you aren't pregnant and you
go into the closet and cry. Unless you've been there, you
don't know how difficult and degrading the examinations
to determine infertility can be—for the man as well as for
the woman. You can't imagine how tense husbands and
wives can get with one another, picking on little things
because they don't want to acknowledge their big concern. I didn't want any more of that. I wanted to do something positive for a change. So I picked one agency, the

best-publicized private adoption agency in our area, and I drove downtown to see about adoption one day.

"I didn't realize then that I was embarking on a lengthy procedure that had tension built into it from its inception. But this time it was worth it, because that's the agency that gave us Andy." Andy is the Matthews' eight-year-old son—tall and blond as is Vicki, and outgoing—his mother's son in many ways. . . . But Andy is at the end of the story, just about, and we left Vicki driving downtown for the first of many visits to the agency, which was the beginning.

That first day, Vicki spent no more than five minutes inside the building, an imposing structure without even a discreet title plaque to mark it, outside, as an adoption agency. Three times, she checked the building's address with that on the paper she'd brought with her. Finally, she found the courage to open the outer door. She had come to the right place. Inside, a receptionist gave Vicki a preliminary form to be filled out and made an appointment for Vicki and Owen to attend a group orientation meeting.

Twelve couples were present at that meeting. The assistant director of the agency made some welcoming remarks followed by what she termed "a realistic picture of adoption today." Even then, in the sixties, there were fewer white, perfect infants than in the past. Even then the agency spokeswoman was beginning to encourage prospective adopters to consider other kinds of children, perhaps those with slight handicaps.

The speaker indicated that the couples would do well to look carefully into their motives for adopting, that both marital partners would have to come to grips with this question, and that among reasons for adoption not considered valid by the agency staff were: to increase a couple's odds of having their "own" child at some future date; to save a marriage.

What about working mothers? "We think it advisable
that a woman take at least a six-month leave of absence
from any job so that she and the baby can get to know
and adjust to one another," said the agency executive.
The Matthews later learned the agency position was less
tolerant of a working mother than that statement would
have led one to believe. Both ambitious young people,
they were fortunate to have met another couple with
similar careers and ideas ("Carbon copies of us," according to Owen) who had expressed honestly their aims and
ambitions to the social worker who then turned down
their application. "We don't give our babies to baby
sitters," were her exact words. Owen and Vicki are convinced this little story worked to their advantage later.

Included in the orientation meeting was a discussion of
the agency process, and of fees, set up on a sliding scale
based on income. At this agency, the scale went from
$100 to $2,000. The speaker stressed that these amounts,
which were negotiable, were fees to cover services and
were not to be construed as payment for a child. She went
on to state that no applications would be accepted that
evening. Instead, all present were to go home and think
about whether they wanted to go ahead. If so, the next
step was to phone for a personal interview and come into
agency "intake," which included monthly family meetings
plus individual screening interviews, diagnostic in nature,
in which each person would "be encouraged to discover
what he is like and what kind of child he can realistically
handle."

"It is likely that no more than half of you who are
present tonight will receive a child from our agency,"
the speaker concluded. "We don't sit in judgment of you,
but we do try to help *you* judge whether adoption is your
right answer." As a caseworker at another agency with
a similar process phrased it, "We select couples out and
encourage formal application from those who seem likely

prospects." Those who sit at the opposite end of the table, the ones who've been helped to "select themselves out," have a different view. They call it "playing God."

√"Suddenly," Owen recalls, "this nice group of people who'd been smiling at one another, united in mutual discomfort, became distinct individuals who eyed each other suspiciously: 'Will I be eliminated?' . . . 'Will that man and woman be given a child?' No longer allies, we'd become contenders for the big prize: a baby. It was a very unpleasant feeling."

The Matthews went home from that meeting, did not ponder their decision, made the required phone call, and went into intake. They discovered that their exhaustive medical examinations, particularly the report from the fertility clinic, worked in their favor. It was proof that they hadn't come to the idea of adoption easily. They had tried to have their own child.

✗Asked to state her feeings about her career, which is important to her, Vicki gave her rehearsed response: "I enjoy my work and derive a lot of satisfaction from it, but not so much that I wouldn't give it up for the chance to be a mother, which is even more important to me."

How had their families reacted to the news of their planned adoption, the caseworker wanted to know. "My folks came around to it slowly," said Owen. This was true. When told of the Matthews' decision to adopt, Owen's mother had cried. "Are you *sure?*" she asked time and time again. She was saddened by their failure to conceive. Vicki's family was equally unhappy. "You have to see how my folks dote on Andy now," Vicki says, "to realize the foolishness of their initial reaction." The interviews were helpful in that they made the couple face honestly the idea of an adopted child, to narrow their definition to a real child rather than an amorphous concept. Vicki had begun her first interview with the statement, "We'll take a child of either sex, up to a year old."

An Oriental child? "Of course." The agency had custody
of a healthy youngster of Puerto Rican parentage. Vicki
was surprised to hear Owen reject the child. He claims he
was equally unprepared for his response, had hoped he
wouldn't have to be put to the test. "No," Owen said. "I
couldn't do it."

"I know I could have accepted a child of another race,"
said Vicki. "But I also knew that I had no right to talk
Owen into a child. This wasn't going to be *my* son; he
was going to be *ours*. It was essential that we both be
happy with our decision." Until the caseworker pointed
it out to them, neither realized they'd begun to speak of
a future child as "he." When asked to think about that,
they recognized their preference for a boy. "That was one
thing adoption had over natural parenthood," Owen said.
"We were able to choose the sex of our child."

Looking back, Owen and Vicki Matthews feel the interviews went well, although at the time they were taking
place the couple was uncertain. Vicki wondered what
Owen had said during his hour with the social worker;
Owen was concerned that he'd conflicted his wife's testi-
mony. In fact, the caseworker had spent more time in-
terrogating each on his or her individual childhood than
on their marital relationship. "Each time she takes leave
of you, the caseworker says, 'I'll call you,'" Vicki mentioned. "It's like dating a fellow and he says he'll phone
you and you sit around on Monday night wondering if
he really meant it, if the phone will ring. It's a very tense
situation. The fact that our initial caseworker left the
agency while we were in process and we had to adjust to
a new personality—and she to us—didn't help matters
either."

When the worker made an appointment for a home
visit, the Matthews were told they'd been provisionally
accepted by the agency. If no untoward information
turned up, they could expect to receive a child. "How I

cleaned that apartment," recalled Vicki. "I'm a competent homemaker, certainly not what you'd call a star in the kitchen, but I even baked a pie. The visit turned out very pleasant: the crust didn't fall, there were no calamities, and we began to think of the worker as our ally. When she left, she told us she would now take her file on us to the other side of the agency, the section that dealt with the children, and try to match us with a suitable youngster. While they no longer were concerned with physical matching, the staff members still attempted to match intellectual and creative capabilities of the child, based on knowledge of his biological parents, with achievements of the adoptive parents. We didn't have to take the first child offered us, our worker stressed. For whatever reason, we would have one chance to reject a child.

"It was a Tuesday when the call came," Vicki Matthews went on. "I remember I had the afternoon off, and so I was lucky to be at home. There was a boy—that was the message. He was three months old; he was healthy. He'd been born out of wedlock to a seventeen-year-old coed. His father was a music student. We could see the child Thursday morning."

Vicki was scheduled to assist at a dance class on Thursday. She called to say she wouldn't be able to make it, sorry, could they get someone else. That call is clear in her mind because it was the first call she made. Only after she hung up did she phone Owen with the news. He was then working for the record company. He arranged to take one week's vacation.

The next day, Vicki and Owen raced around town, buying crib, bassinet, layette for a three-month-old baby. They made arrangements with a diaper service. They borrowed a carriage from a friend whose child had outgrown it, for they had been told, if all went well, they could take the baby home with them. (Some agencies customarily leave a two- to three-day period between

"viewing" and "taking home" in case, in the words of one
agency director, "the couple gets cold feet.")

Owen and Vicki Matthews expected all to go well.
After all they'd been through to get to this moment, what
could make them turn down a child? (One couple who
did reject a baby they'd come prepared to take home
with them made their decision when a medical checkup
of the infant, on the same day the little boy was to be
placed, revealed a heart murmur. When this new information was related, the husband and wife rationalized that
the time demands of their separate careers wouldn't permit them to give the best possible care and attention to a
handicapped child, and decided not to take the baby.
The neighborhood children, assembled to greet the new
baby, were disappointed when the couple returned home,
childless and carrying the baby clothes they'd brought
with them to the agency. Five weeks later, the man and
wife were again called to the agency. This time, they
came home with a baby girl. The mother remains guilt-
ridden, wondering, "What ever happened to the little
boy?" and "If I'd given birth to a child with a heart murmur, wouldn't it have been my responsibility to care for
him?")

Owen and Vicki were fortunate. They didn't have to
make such a decision. The male infant whom they met at
the agency building on Thursday morning was healthy,
alert, and "just beautiful" according to his new parents.
"You don't know what to expect of the moment of meeting your child," Owen said. "You just know this is it, this
is the child that will be mine, a real baby and not the
child of my fantasy. I later learned you can experience the
same thoughts when you view your biologic child."

The baby had been brought from his foster home earlier
that morning (the Matthews did not meet his foster
mother) and looked about ready for his nap. "Why
don't you give him his bottle?" asked the caseworker,

who sensed Vicki's insecurity and wanted to give her something positive to do.

After the baby had been fed, Owen and Vicki handed the caseworker the clothes they'd brought for the infant. Then some lovely lady—a nurse? another worker? Vicki can't recall—took the child away and changed his clothing while his parents-to-be were given information on his habits (the hours of waking, napping, going to bed for the night), his diet, and several bottles of milk-based formula. He was not yet on whole milk.

Then they went home, knowing there was a six-month probation period when they could give up the child or, if cause was shown, have the child taken from them. Throughout this time they'd be in contact with their social worker, whose role was to support the new parents as they made their adjustment to familyhood. During the six months, the Matthews were to report any serious illness to the caseworker, were to request permission if they planned to take the baby out of state. When the half year was up, a date would be set for a hearing at family or surrogate's court where the adoption would be finalized.

In most classic adoption stories, "The End" could be written here, for the family then goes on to live its life, with the variations of joy, frustration, and sorrow that are part of most biographies, but with the exception that this is the story of an adoptive family who will have special problems of identity that will have to be dealt with over the years. The variable here is that Vicki did indeed become pregnant, *and* during the six-month period of probation.

After the shock wore off, Vicki experienced a strong feeling of fear. Since she was going to give birth to a child, would Andy be taken from her? Owen and she debated the merits of not telling the caseworker the news, of trying to conceal Vicki's condition until after the adoption was finalized. "By this time," Owen says, "I had

learned the meaning of father love. Andy was ours, and
we couldn't bear the thought of giving him up, not even
if it meant that Vicki would have to abort the baby she
was carrying, as miraculous as this pregnancy seemed
to be. To think, we'd even considered that possibility.
Luckily, we decided to tell the social worker the truth and
you know what she said? 'Congratulations!'" Owen and
Vicki are today the proud parents of Andy, eight, and
Leonard, seven. Andy's the one who's a dead ringer for
his mother.

Today, this tale of the adoption of a healthy infant
child may be looked on as historical romance. Fewer
such adoptions are taking place. The pages in the note-
books of caseworkers are being filled with information on
transracial placement, homes for the handicapped, locating parents for young people long past the age of diapers
—in short, adoptions such as those described in the chapters that follow.

Transracial Adoption

As the concerned public and many professional workers in adoption agencies began to abandon the criterion of sameness—no longer matching blue-eyed infant to blue-eyed adult—they inadvertently were preparing the way for the next step in the process of opening homes to children who wait: transracial adoption. The term generally denotes placement of black and racially mixed children in white homes, which is how we use it here. Some agencies, however, use "transracial" to define placement of a black child in a white home and "interracial" to mean placing a child of mixed racial background in a white home, or either kind of child in a mixed home.

While this newly prominent feature on the face of adoption is viewed by many as revolutionary change, it has in fact evolved slowly and steadily, beginning with interracial placement.

There always has been some trickling in of babies to the United States from foreign countries—black-market infants, older children rescued from nations devastated by war and natural disaster. In the 1950s, the trickle became a stream when some 2,300 Korean children were brought to the United States, largely through the efforts of a dedi-

cated—and controversial—Oregon farmer, Harry Holt,
and placed in white American homes. Most of these children were of mixed race, born to Korean women and
fathered by American servicemen. Looked upon with dis-
favor by the Koreans, a race-proud people, they were
abandoned by their fathers and unwanted by their
mothers, in many cases because their mothers feared they
would be unable to care for the children. American homes
welcomed them. To this date, their number has grown to
more than 7,000 including full Koreans whose needs for
parents and permanent homes were recognized and met.
Thousands more orphaned or abandoned children have
been brought by volunteer organizations to the United
States for adoption from Japan, Taiwan, Thailand, Hong
Kong, and, recently and in fewer numbers, South Vietnam.
Most of these children have been adopted by Caucasian
families.

At the same time, in the decade 1958–68, four hundred Indian children were placed for adoption, mostly
with Caucasian parents, in a project sponsored jointly by
the Child Welfare League of America and the Bureau of
Indian Affairs, Department of the Interior. While these
programs were under way, a greater number of family-
less and needy black and mixed-race youngsters within
our borders remained unrecognized.

Howard and Ann Partridge, a white Connecticut couple who adopted two Korean children, the second born
with a cleft palate, before they added a four-year-old
black son from New York's Harlem to their growing
family, speak to the problem. "You may wonder why we
went halfway across the globe for our first two children
before we responded to the needs of youngsters who were
right in our own backyard," says Ann. "It's not that we
were prejudiced in favor of Oriental children—or any-
color children. We *were* seeking youngsters who needed
us, who might otherwise remain homeless. Why hadn't

we looked in the eastern urban centers of our own country? The answer is simple . . . and appalling: we just didn't know the children were there."

The discovery of the seemingly obvious in the case of the Partridges is in microcosm the problem that existed nationwide. The first significant steps in the placement of minority-race youngsters—a program that continues to affect the course of adoption in the United States today— were taken in Montreal, Canada, in the late 1950s. Mrs. Muriel B. McCrea, former director of the Children's Service Centre, Montreal, now retired, described the history of that first program, which was inaugurated by the center working in conjunction with Montreal's Open Door Society, a dynamic group of parents who have done much to further the cause of adoption in general and interracial adoption in particular.

"It had never struck us until the spring of 1958," Mrs. McCrea recounted in a speech delivered to the Frontiers in Adoption seminar held in Michigan nearly ten years later, "that we had in the body of our children 187 Negro children who were legally adoptable whom we had never done anything about. At this point we had about ten homes for every white child: we had so many homes we were giving them away to Nova Scotia and other provinces. We had been placing children with physical and emotional handicaps since 1940. So we literally had not a child in the agency who was free for adoption who was not placed for adoption. And yet we had 187 Negro children that we had never even looked at as adoptable."

When Mrs. McCrea and her staff began to look about them, they were dismayed at what they found: the unmarried parents' department had not been bothering to get consent for adoption from a Negro mother at all. This wasn't in any stated policy of the agency. It was just accepted as a foregone conclusion that they were not going to get homes for the children anyway, so why bother to get the consent. When a Negro mother came to ask for adoption care for her child or for placement for her child, she was told the agency could provide boarding care, but that no adoption would be possible. Was it any wonder that so many black mothers elected to keep their out-of-wedlock babies?

Recognition of those children who *had* been surrendered wasn't enough to assure their placements, nor were the considerable publicity and community relations efforts put forth by the agency people and members of the organization. At the end of that first year, they had found homes for only three children, while the number of children available had climbed to 242. Further analysis revealed that while the agency had ventured into new territory, it had continued to employ traditional methods, matching available child to possible parent. Only when they began to present the mixed-race child to all parents applying for a child as an available youngster needing love and nurture rather than prejudging whether the parents would accept a child who looked different from themselves did they meet with any success. The families met the challenge. "We learned something about ourselves through this program," stated Mrs. McCrea. "The greatest reservations through all the time we have worked with the program have been on the part of the social worker."

This once unthinkable practice has grown in numbers and acceptance. A nationwide survey conducted by the Opportunity Division of the Boys and Girls Aid Society of Oregon reported more than 2,500 black placements in white homes for 1971, a tremendous increase over the 733 such placements made only four years earlier. Further findings are that transracial adoption accounted for 35 per cent of all black children placed in 1971. Yet white parents who seek to adopt across racial lines still find they have to contend with the attitudes and reservations of the individual social worker.

The experience of Michael and Sandra Thomason comes closer to being the rule than the exception. Michael, forty-two, and Sandra, thirty-eight, are the parents of two biological children: Joy, now twelve, and Michael, Jr., nine. When Joy was six years old, Sandra became pregnant for the third time. Because this had not been a planned pregnancy, Sandra was surprised to find herself extremely despondent when it ended in miscarriage. She had begun to look forward to a new baby in her life. She and Michael then decided to try to conceive another child, and they did. A second miscarriage followed.

Fate intervened in the form of a leaflet that had been slipped under the front door of the six-room garden apartment the Thomasons inhabit in a government-subsidized middle-income development. In this integrated community, the leaflet was perhaps meant to appeal to the black residents of the house. Beneath a picture of a wide-eyed black baby, the text read, "Can you find room in your family for the children who wait?" The copy went on to speak of the availability for adoption of black and mixed-race children, and urged anyone interested to contact the renowned private adoption agency whose address and phone number were given.

Michael and Sandra discussed adoption in general and specifically warmed to the idea of a black child. As parents of two healthy youngsters, they felt that God would have wanted them to adopt a child who might not otherwise find a home. Although not conscientious do-gooders, the couple is active in their church. Conscience rules much of their action—a quality they seem to share with many families who seek to adopt children with special needs. The couple's children, Joy and young Michael, were consulted; they expressed pleasure in the idea. Their parents called the agency and made an appointment to meet with a social worker.

"When we first met with our worker," Sandra recalls,

"she asked what kind of child we wanted. I told her a black child. She immediately translated that into 'mixed race.' She could not accept the idea that we really didn't care if the child had kinky hair or very dark skin or whatever. We wanted a healthy child—we agonized over that decision because we knew there were handicapped youngsters needing homes, but I didn't feel prepared to cope with problems of health, mental or physical—and we wanted a black child.

"Did we realize what we were doing, the worker kept asking. She intimated that any adopted child could not be as bright as our biologic offspring and that we'd be unhappy about that." Sandra nods in the direction of Cara, the black child the Thomasons located through the services of a municipal agency they applied to the day they were rejected by the private agency, and who is now their daughter. "Now take a look at that child. She's Miss Brains." Cara is a bright-eyed, chubby little three year old who moves with confidence around the cluttered apartment, jabbering all the while as she goes.

"Our first social worker also warned us that if we adopted a black baby, our 'own' children might be rejected in some social circles," Michael adds. "Remember, she was a representative of the agency that was publicizing the need to locate homes for black children."

"And anyway," interjects blond-haired Joy, who has been sitting with us throughout the discussion, "I wouldn't want to be part of any circle that didn't accept my black sister." Joy is very protective of Cara.

It took about five months from the time the Thomasons applied to the city agency to the day they received Cara —"after a lot of ritual and bureaucracy," according to Sandra, but all things considered a shorter wait than most couples experience. Even those personnel who approve of mixed-race placements like to give a couple time to think through their decision, to realize they're adopting one child rather than an entire cause, and to be quite certain of their desire to care for that one child—walking the baby in the wee hours of the morning rather than setting out on a week-long civil rights march.

Cara was eight months old when the Thomasons brought her home. She had spent three months of her life in a hospital after birth, not because she was in ill health but as a holding action, and then five months in foster care. "She was very overweight," says Michael, bringing forth a Polaroid snapshot to prove his point, "and she couldn't eat from a spoon. We know nothing about the kind of home she had been in, but we do know that she could drink from a soda bottle when she came to us, and she became excited when she spied a can of beer. She could drink from that, too. She also knew what potato chips were. But she was a happy, warm child, so we do know she wasn't mistreated." Cara—and the Thomasons —were lucky. Many children come to their adoptive homes with an unhappy history which they recall only in nightmares and which their new parents feel helpless to attack, not knowing the specifics of mistreatment. Cara adjusted to her new home at once.

The neighbors in the development seemed to adjust to Cara's presence without effort and with genuine good-will. Some noted "what a wonderful thing" the Thomasons were doing, which Sandra and Michael translate into "how noble of you." "There's nothing noble about adopting a child," says Sandra. "Cara isn't our pet project. She's our child. Look what she has done for us as a family."

Indeed, the Thomasons are a close-knit, child-centered family. Michael comes home at six each evening from his job as a computer programer to have dinner with the children. Four mornings a week, during the hours when the older children are in school, Sandra leaves Cara at a day care center near the community center in which she works, part-time, as secretary and all-around general helper—a girl Friday, as it were, except that Friday is the one weekday she has off.

Vacations and holidays are spent with friends rather than relatives. Michael's mother has steadfastly refused to accept an adopted grandchild—of any color, she claims, although Michael has doubts about that over-all indictment, believing that his mother's rejection has to do with nothing as much as racial prejudice, so the family has severed connections with the lady. Sandra's parents live halfway across the country, therefore feel less threatened by the adoption. Sandra and Michael were pleased when Sandra's mother acknowledged Cara's recent birthday with a carefully chosen doll—black—and a greeting card signed, "Happy birthday from your adopted grandma."

"Isn't that strange?" queried Michael, Jr., ingenuously. "Grandma's not adopted."

His father's sister, Aunt Laraine, whom they saw infrequently in the past, no longer is a visitor. The few times she was asked to dinner, she would arrive at the Thomasons' apartment, kiss the older children and pointedly ignore Cara. When told, "Cara's our child; you'll have to treat her just as you do our other children or you'll see none of them," Laraine stopped coming. That incident took place more than a year ago.

Interviews with many white couples who have adopted across racial lines indicate that while conflict with a family member, neighbor or business associate does not follow the adoption as a rule, reactions such as Sandra and Michael met with are not the exception. A study of characteristics of 186 white couples who have adopted black or racially mixed children has shown them to be of a higher socioeconomic level than most families, to have religious or humanitarian motives and to be isolated from their families and detached from their communities.

One Midwestern couple, parents of three biologic

children and two adopted youngsters—the first, a girl
born with a club foot; the second, a healthy black boy—
told of their next-door neighbor who was so excited following the adoption of the boy (she had not ceased
praising them for having adopted a handicapped daughter), she phoned and asked if she could come by to see
the baby moments after the man and wife drove up to
their home, a blanket-swaddled infant tenderly held in
the mother's arms. "Your new baby . . . how wonderful,"
the neighbor enthused as she came hurrying through the
front doorway. Then . . . pause. No one had informed her
the new baby would be black. Two years have passed,
during which time this lady has stayed safely on her side
of the shrubbery separating the properties.

"Sometimes," says Clayton Hagen, former supervisor
of adoptions for Minnesota's Lutheran Social Services,
"we feel we ought to focus our efforts to educate the public to an understanding and acceptance of adoption not
on the prospective adoptive parents but on neighbors and
on friends of the grandmother." Much grandparental re-
sistance is based upon fear of what the neighbors will say,
which is why, as in the case of the Thomasons, long-
distance relatives tend to seem the most understanding.

Sandra Thomason sees as most supportive the friends
the family has made within their housing complex who,
because they are an amalgam of races and religions, are
accepting of the multiracial family, which means that
just as they don't condemn the arrangement, they also
manage not to gush over the adopted child as a bit of local exotica. Parents who adopt transracially find this excessive attention almost—but not quite—as distressing as
rejection. They see the over-reaction as an attempt to underline the acceptance—"We really do approve of your
black child, honestly"—as though the overenthusers really
are trying to reassure themselves as to the merits of the
situation. But the child in the spotlight becomes spoiled,

begins to think he is extra special. Where there are other children in the family, too much attention to the adopted child causes them to resent the new sibling. More than one parent has been faced with a tearful plea to "Send him back, please," which is heard in many a household following the arrival of a new baby—by biologic means or otherwise—but to which the adoptive parent reacts with greater sensitivity. Adoptive parents simply want to be able to raise their children normally.

Michael and Sandra believe that black children in white homes can be raised most normally and successfully in an integrated neighborhood, where they will meet with others of their race daily and not be brought up as black persons in an all-white world. "*I* don't feel white, whatever that's supposed to be," says Cara's mother, "and so when I look at Cara I don't see black. First, I see my daughter. She's so much a part of me, there are times I look at her and wonder that she didn't come out of me. Then I realize she is a separate person with a separate identity, and that I have a responsibility to make her like and respect herself, which includes respect for her status as a black person in America."

Voices have been raised within both the white and black communities that say this cannot be done. In some cases, the naysayers speak from the vantage point of prejudice; in others, from a sincere feeling that white adoptive parents could not possibly understand a black child's world in a racist society nor adequately prepare that child to function in that society as a black adult.

Meeting in Nashville in April 1972, the National Association of Black Social Workers went on record as being "in vehement opposition" to the placement of black children with white families. Because their position paper continues to provoke great controversy among the many people concerned with adoption today, professional social workers, adoptive parents and laymen, much of the paper bears quoting.

> We have taken the position that Black children should be placed only with Black families whether in foster care or for adoption. Black children belong, physically, psychologically and culturally, in Black families in order that they receive the total sense of themselves and develop a sound projection of their future. Human beings are products of their environment and develop their sense of values, attitudes and self concept within their family structures. Black children in white homes are cut off from the healthy development of themselves as Black people.
>
> Our position is based on:
>
> 1. the necessity of self-determination from birth to death of all Black people;
>
> 2. the need of our young ones to begin at birth to identify with all Black people in a Black community;
>
> 3. the philosophy that we need our own to build a strong nation.
>
> The socialization process for every child begins at birth. Included in the socialization process is the child's cultural heritage which is an important segment of the total process. This must begin at the earliest moment, otherwise our children will not have the background and knowledge which is necessary to survive in a racist society. This is impossible if the child is placed with white parents in a white environment.
>
> White institutions have repeatedly stated that they are using new methods to find "good" Black homes; white institutions lack the ability to determine a "good" black home. This violates our rights as a group of people to determine our own destiny and ignores the Black family as an institution with legitimate values of its own. . . .

This issue was further developed at the Third North American Conference on Adoptable Children, which was held in St. Louis later that same month. The Black Caucus reaffirmed its position that "Black children *must* only be

placed with Black families," further stating their belief
that any agency that placed a child transracially because
it could not find him a black family simply hadn't worked
very hard to find that black family. Said one member off
the record, "You may be willing to adopt a black son, but
what it all comes down to is: would you want him to
marry your white daughter?"

A good number of the 675 delegates to the convention
had at some time been forced to face up to that question
or others which were essentially similar. White parents of
black and mixed-race youngsters, they reacted emotionally to the statement issued by the black organization.
This comment by a member of the California delegation
is typical of the feelings of the adoptive parents groups:
"While I agree with their [NABSW's] position on the
need to find black homes for black children, I don't believe enough homes are available *now*, and it infuriates
me to be accused of hurting my black son. He will have
problems as he grows to adulthood—probably more than
most, since he is both adopted and a member of a transracial household—but he will not have the problems of a
child brought up without a family to support him. He
can turn to us and, since we love him, he will know that
he can rely on our support."

An Iowa farmer, the father of four tall, blond, crew-
cut sons born to him and his fair-haired wife and of two
black, Afro-coiffed, adopted daughters, reacted with as-
surance. "The black social workers may be working to
create a situation where blacks go to blacks or nowhere,"
he said firmly, "but we'll be working steadfastly in the
opposite direction. And I think we'll win."

Yet another, similar response may be found in the writ-
ings of David Anderson, the Caucasian adoptive father
of three interracial children. In his book on interracial
adoption, *Children of Special Value,* Anderson makes the
point that, of course, some parents who've adopted trans-

racially will do a better job of raising their children than others, sometimes for reasons that have to do with their race and sometimes for reasons that don't. But of this he feels fairly certain: "A black child who grows up with white parents who have a strong commitment to the idea of his blackness, and who incorporate such a commitment in their creation of a strong family, stands a far better chance of developing a healthy sense of personal and racial pride than does a black child who grows up without any parents at all."

It is the black social workers' contention that black children should remain in foster homes and institutions rather than be placed in the homes of willing white families that causes the greatest furor, even among those people who are working toward the goal of a black home for every waiting black child. For most people concerned with adoption today, the word "institution" is anathema.

"This is the most destructive position that could be taken," according to Dr. James L. Curtis, a black psychiatrist at the Cornell University Medical College, who rebutted the association's position in a New York *Times* interview. "The practice in this field is almost uniform in believing that a child has a right to grow up in an adoptive home if one can at all be obtained for him. It seems that the black social workers' position could only lend support to the more reactionary and bigoted agencies and agency practices."

One of the results of the pressure brought to bear on the established agencies by NABSW is that increased effort is being expended to locate more black homes and it is meeting with success. This has carried over to other minority groups, so that efforts are being made to locate Oriental parents for Oriental youngsters, Puerto Rican families for Puerto Rican children, and so on. A second result, however, is just what Dr. Curtis feared. Opportunity's 1972 survey found a decrease of 39 per cent from the previous year in placements of black children in white families, which was not offset by significantly greater placements, nationwide, of black children in black families. Some agencies that formerly made transracial placements have ceased to do so, even when they cannot place a child within his racial background. As they play games of color politics, actual children are the pawns, and it is they who continue to lose even after the players themselves have gone on to other pastimes. One Caucasian couple who had successfully adopted a child of mixed race via an established Southern agency found that reaction had set in at the very agency that had welcomed their initial application. When they recently decided the time had come for them to enlarge their family, the woman of the house placed a call to their former caseworker. "We'd like to adopt another child," the mother said—just that, no more. She didn't specify age, sex, state of health or color.

"Sorry," came the clipped reply. "We have no white babies or white children of any age."

As though she were shopping, the woman claims she felt like responding, "If you're out of white, I'll take rye or even pumpernickel. What I'm really interested in is bread." Instead she heard herself calmly inquire, "What children *are* available?"

"Black children."

"Then I'd like to make application to adopt a black child."

"Sorry," said the agency person. "We're only accepting applications for black children from black families." Click.

Under a new policy adopted in July 1973, the State of Illinois will place black children under its guardianship for adoption only with black families. In November 1972, the Child Welfare League of America amended its standard on transracial adoptions to read: "While we specifically affirm transracial adoptions as one means of achieving needed permanence for some children, we recognize that other things being equal in today's social climate, it is preferable to place a child in a family of his own racial background."

New York City's Division of Adoption Services is one agency that continues to consider all applicants for available children. "We try very hard to find black parents for black children," says its director, M. Mae Neely. "With our recruitment we go to the black community and we try to reach black people through the media. The response is impressive. Nevertheless, we haven't enough black families for those children awaiting placement right now. In the meantime, we must work with all families—white and black—who can provide good homes for available children."

"In the meantime" . . . "Until enough black homes become available" . . . "Preferable to an institution" . . . Phrases such as these run through the statements of those who stand in favor of transracial placement as a means of adoption. Clearly, the greater community is saying, this form of adoption must be seen as second best, any adoptive home in a storm, with the pot of gold at rainbow's end a black home for a black child, white home for a white child, a possible sequence retrogressing to blond-haired child for blond-haired grownup.

Minnesota's Clayton Hagen finds fault with such exclusive, and exclusionary, policies of placement and with the very idea that any child should find himself in a home considered, by both adoption worker and adoptive parent, as second best. This second-best attitude is potentially harmful, he feels, in that it causes those white parents who are raising black children to do so on the defensive, their defense being that their child is with them because there were no black parents for him. In their attempts to help their child develop an identity that is different from theirs, they may lack the spontaneous and natural relationship that can exist between child and parent. A more important identity question must be raised before there is any move to adopt transracially. "If a person sees his identity in his race," says Hagen, "he cannot be parent to a child of another. However, a person who finds his identity as a human being can well be parent to another human being." He questions the assumption that black children belong with black parents and submits that interracial adoption is valid on its own merits.

At Lutheran Social Services, practice has been to question potential parents about their attitudes so they can better understand their own feelings and decide if they can be parents to a child of another race. "Does a child need to look like you in order for you to be a parent to him?" applicants have been asked. "Must he look like your nationality?"—which is as pertinent in the case of dark-haired parents of Italian heritage faced with a blond-haired baby as well as for white parents considering the adoption of a black child. Couples have been asked to consider: "Would the factors of another race prevent you from calling him son?" . . . "Must he be able to go to college?" On the question of "other people," Clayton Hagen says, "Our question is not what other people will say but: how do you feel about what other people say, whether stranger, neighbor, or your own parents?" Sandra and Michael Thomason reacted to rejection of Cara by severing relations with family members they deemed racist. Not all couples could, or would be willing to, do this.

The point of Clayton Hagen's approach has been to make couples come to grips with the realities of their request, to educate nonparents to the meaning of parenthood as well as to dissuade people who seek to adopt with a romantic view of the "good" they will be doing rather than a realistic view of what parenthood actually entails.

With no tradition to guide the couple seeking to adopt

across racial lines nor any significant studies evaluating the long-range effects of such placement on the children involved,* the important question Hagen asks is, "Can you give another individual a feeling of being a person of worth and value, and help him, in turn, to value and respond to others?" If one can do this, he suggests, perhaps this is all we need to know now. "If the child has a good concept of himself, he can then meet all the problems we fear he will encounter and not be overcome. If he does not have a good concept of himself, any problem may be too much."

* The Child Welfare League of America is embarked on such a study at the present time. It is to be completed by August 1974.

Adoption in the Black Community

Just as the black child for so long had been looked upon by agency people as unadoptable, so the black family had been viewed as not interested in adopting. This, too, is being proven false. For one thing, the black family has historically absorbed many "outside" youngsters without the formality of legal adoption proceedings. Additionally, surveys have shown that blacks adopt in larger proportion than do whites, given their percentage of the total population.

It is also true that there are a large number of black and mixed-race youngsters who need homes. A 1969 study by the Child Welfare League of America found that, in 240 agencies providing racial data on approved homes and children available for adoption, there were 116 approved applications from white homes for every 100 white children available and only 39 nonwhite homes approved for every 100 nonwhite children reported as needing adoptive placement. While the figures concerning the black adoption picture have since improved, with an impressive increase in the number of black children placed, nationwide, in both black and white homes (from 3,122 in 1968 to 7,420 in 1971, according to a survey done

by the Opportunity Division of the Boys and Girls Aid
Society of Oregon), a significant number of black youngsters remain among the children who wait. Thus, additional efforts are being expended to bring even greater
numbers of black families into the adoptive community.

The first step taken in this direction has been for those
responsible for the development of adoption programs
and policies to look at the possible deterrents to application for adoption from black families. In her article on
"Adoption Resources of Black Children" published in
Children, March–April 1971, Ursula M. Gallagher, U. S.
Children's Bureau specialist on adoptions and services to
unmarried parents, listed some of these deterrents as: the
generally lower economic situation of black families as
compared with white; the tendency among some black
families to regard social agencies as a "white man's resource"; an impression that all adoption agencies require
proof of sterility; a reluctance to be questioned about
personal matters; expectance of rejection from having experienced it at every turn in life; anxiety about filling out
required forms; and inability to meet legal fees.

"Friends still can't believe that all it cost us to adopt
Alice was eleven dollars in court fees," says Clementine
Freeman, who, with her husband, Bob, added three-
year-old Alice to a family that already contained two
bio-children: Arthur, age nine, and Amanda, four. The
Freemans are black.

"Bob and I had talked about adopting even before we
were married," says Clementine, "but in the years that
followed we'd heard of some experiences that our acquaintances had been through, and that made us think
again. We know of one couple who adopted a baby boy,
and it cost them eight hundred dollars. Well, we never
had that kind of money." Bob is a hook-and-ladder man
with Detroit's fire department. Clementine works as a
practical nurse.

"And another couple was rejected by a different agency in this city because they weren't religious," Bob adds. "Well, we aren't churchgoers, either. I mean, we believe in God and, Clementine, she goes to church more often than I do, but we haven't got a specific religious affiliation, so we thought no agency was going to look at us as possible parents for any of its kids. Also, we had our own, which we believed would work against us. The way it all turned out, none of that mattered. All that the social worker said to us was, 'We're looking for people who are comfortable with one another and who feel they can love a child.' We were pretty sure we could do that."

The Freemans returned to the idea of adoption in response to a concentrated publicity campaign then being waged in the Detroit community. It stressed the need for black homes for homeless black children of all ages. The 1967 riots had led to a dialogue in this city between the black and white communities in which the needs of the local citizenry were discussed. One glaring need was homes for black children. In 1967 only 93 black children were placed in adoptive homes by thirteen agencies reporting to the United Community Services in Detroit. Percentage-wise, 6.5 per cent of the children placed for adoption were black, but 60 per cent of the illegitimate births were to black unwed mothers.

The community's answer was to create a new agency that would address itself to recruiting black families for these children. Funds were to be supplied by the United Foundation. In May 1969 this new agency opened its doors. Its name announced its purpose: Homes for Black Children.

The first problem its staff had to face was to inform the members of the black community that the path to its door (and to the children beyond) was easy to follow, as well as to undo preconceived notions about "agencies" in general. Early publicity efforts made much of the fact that this agency did not require applicants to be homeowners, to have an income above a stated minimum or to be able to show proof of church attendance. What was clearly announced was that the agency charged no fees to adopting families.

Several interviews with staff members were held on television and radio programs. The publicity piece that drew the greatest response (and the one that attracted the Freemans' attention) was a feature story in a popular weekly column in the Detroit *News*. The column "A Child Is Waiting," tells about a youngster (or family group of children) who needs an adoptive family, and refers interested readers to the agency responsible for that child's placement. One week, women's editor Ruth Carlton featured a black child in her column by way of introducing readers to Homes for Black Children.

Sydney Duncan, the articulate, soft-spoken black director of HBC, recalls that this one article brought an immediate response of fifty applications for the child pictured—which astounded critics who claimed that black families in the area were not interested in adopting. Clementine and Bob Freeman were among those who responded.

While the Freemans did not end up with the child in the newspaper, the secretary who answered their phone inquiry took down their names, address, phone number, and racial identification. (White couples seeking to adopt transracially are referred to other agencies—HBC has not announced itself as opposed to transracial adoption, but sees as its concern working with the black population.) The agency does not send out application forms. The secretary assured the Freemans they would hear from a representative of the agency within two weeks.

Her word was good. Caseworker Lorraine Brown contacted the Freemans before the two weeks were up. She offered to set up an appointment with them at the location of their choice, either at her office or their home. They could be seen by her or join in a series of group intake meetings. They chose to meet Mrs. Brown at her office.

The atmosphere at Homes for Black Children is informal and welcoming. The building, a former private residence located on a corner lot of a street of gracious homes in what is now an all-black neighborhood, bears no resemblance to an official, institutional structure. Local zoning rules prohibit the placement of a sign on the lawn.

Once inside, applicants are greeted by a black secretary who is seated in the cheerful reception room. The door to the director's office beyond is frequently ajar. Staff members visit back and forth with one another, consulting on their individual case loads or simply showing current photographs of the children with whom they're working or of their own youngsters. Many young mothers work at the agency, the associate director herself recently became the adoptive mother of a son, and all the workers but two are black. The two white workers have had extensive experience working with blacks in the inner city.

The informality, and the staff makeup, was purposeful. In a study conducted by Dr. Trudy Festinger, of the New York University School of Social Services, of couples who had withdrawn from the adoption process before having a child placed with them, Dr. Festinger found black families that had contact with white workers were more likely to withdraw than those whose contact had been a black worker. Homes for Black Children was organized to eliminate that rejection factor.

Clementine Freeman recalls the first meeting with Mrs. Brown: "We chatted. It was all so very relaxed—rather jolly, in fact. We had coffee and we talked—mostly about what kind of child we had in mind. Bob and I felt that, while we would accept a boy, we'd prefer a daughter who could be a good friend to Amanda, our four year old. We believed our son Arthur, who was nine, was too old and involved in his own world—his school, the Scouts, his ball club—to spend much time with any new child who would come into the family. Also, I did want a child who was out of diapers. I didn't long to go back to that stage."

Clementine had just begun a planned year's leave of absence from her job because she felt the need of rest and some more time to spend with her family (Bob's schedule has him spending alternate weeks on night duty), and so she and Bob thought that, if ever they were going to do something about adopting a child, this was the year for it.

At the end of the meeting, Mrs. Brown gave the Freemans some papers to be filled out (medicals, employment verifications, and three references are required) and offered to help them with the forms if they ran into any difficulties. If all went well, she indicated, she hoped to place a child with them no later than ten weeks beyond the completion of the home study, which could take as little as six to eight weeks.

There is no typical length of time between application and placement. Sometimes, it's difficult for a family to assemble the necessary papers. Many are missing such documents as birth certificates, a copy of their marriage license, or a death certificate of a deceased spouse. The workers at HBC sometimes must spend a great deal of their time helping families learn how to obtain these papers. They've found that almost any black person who was born in the South more than thirty years ago has a birth certificate problem. If an otherwise qualified couple cannot become parents for lack of a document, the worker tries to obtain affidavits or other types of verification. Thus, many families who had been turned down by other agencies or who didn't pursue their interest in adoption because they feared failure were enabled to adopt children.

Since the Freemans did have all their papers intact, were in good health, and had established a good rapport with their caseworker (had this not been the case, they might have been offered a change of caseworker), and because there then was a backlog of children to be placed, they had reason to assume all would go well and that soon—sooner than they'd anticipated—there'd be a new child in their home. They decided to tell their respective families of their plan.

"My father's reaction was, 'You're crazy. You can't afford it,'" said Bob. "He was worried about the money part, but since I wasn't coming to him for money there was nothing he could do but try to reason with me. I respect my parents, but I've been a man for a long time now.

"I wasn't so concerned about the money," Bob went on. "I figured that Alice would share Amanda's room, and clothes have never been that much of a problem, but for shoes. Clementine makes almost all the kids' clothing, except for Arthur's slacks, and we're not at all fussy about accepting hand-me-downs from friends. And how much can a little girl eat? So I told my father I thought we could handle it."

Clementine's mother worried more about "the hereditary part—did we know what kind of child we were getting," according to her daughter.

"The way I look at it," said Bob, "a child's a child. I know what county this little girl was born in, and I know a couple of young fellows that got girls pregnant in that county, and for all I know Alice's father could have been a distant relative of mine. I'm not going to sit around and worry about blood."

Eight weeks later, the Freemans were introduced to Alice and spent some time chatting with her—more accurately, they watched as she played with some toys placed about a small recreation room. Alice was not an outgoing child. Neither was she sullen. "She seemed like a nice little girl—it's hard to remember, she's such a chatterbox now—but I didn't think anything like 'I really love her' or 'I don't care for her,'" Clementine thinks back. "It was more that I knew she was to be mine and I wanted her home."

The next week, Alice came home to stay. "She was still shy and wouldn't hold on to either of us," Bob related. "We had bought her a bag of Fritos, and she clutched it all the way home. The first person she warmed up to was Amanda. She walked over to her and offered her a chip, and wouldn't you know—Amanda bit her finger." Alice cried out and ran to Clementine for comfort.

"She called me Mommy and Bob, Daddy, right away. She picked that up from the other children," Clementine continued. "And that was that. Mrs. Brown told us she was ready to work with us right through that first year, until the adoption was finalized, and any time afterward if we felt we had any problems, but there weren't any. I hate to think that Arthur or Amanda could go into a new home situation as easily as Alice did. But she did—and that's the truth."

Since Alice came to live with them, two acquaintances of the Freemans have adopted youngsters through the agency. One adopted an infant; the other, an older boy. Sarah and Daniel Greene, who adopted the boy, Philip, seven, had been feeling "dissatisfied" since their three children, all in their twenties, had established their separate lives and moved out of the Greenes' comfortable, spacious home. Something was missing. After the Freemans added Alice to their family and told them how pleasant the entire experience had been, the Greenes admitted to one another that the something missing in their lives was a child. They were kept active with other people's children—they belong to a hiking club and the group takes several trips a year, but when the Greenes returned home they found too much room and too much quiet. Mrs. Greene was forty-five (had she not told me so, I would have guessed her to be in her mid-thirties) and her husband three years her senior, and they didn't believe any agency would consider them.

Encouraged by the Freemans, Sarah Greene phoned Homes for Black Children one day. Her experience was not so different from that described for the Freemans except that the Greenes came home with a son. "I call him 'my company keeper,'" says Sarah. "We go downtown together every Saturday afternoon, to the library or to the stores. Or we go to a children's movie. We even went to Florida last summer and took Philip to Disneyland. We had a ball. We just enjoy him so. And so do my older children. They come around to visit more often than they did before we had Philip, or they'll just phone and ask, 'How's my kid brother?' They think he's a toy, except for my older daughter, who has two of her own now. She knows that children are work, too. But they're worth it."

Bob Greene claims he feels younger, less tired since he became the father of a young son. "I used to take a lot of Geritol," he comments. "I have no need for that kind of pick-me-up now."

Sarah Greene's sister and her husband, who spent twenty married years as a childless couple, have also adopted a son from Homes for Black Children.

"Our adoptive parents are our best advertisement," says Sydney Duncan. "That's why we're so concerned about how we deal with everyone who comes to us. It's also the reason behind our never charging a fee for our services, not even to those families who can well afford it. Say we're dealing with a couple that earns forty thousand dollars a year and we charge them one thousand, which is okay with them. They run into friends at a party who express interest in adopting and who ask what the entire procedure costs. They're told, 'One thousand dollars.' Eventually, that bit of information will filter down to a less affluent group and it might come out something like, 'I hear they charge you a thousand dollars to adopt a child at that agency.' Do you see what I'm driving at? While we cut across all lines of religion, class, and economics in the black community, our average adoptive client works in the automobile factories and makes assembly-line pay. That can be pretty good, with overtime, but there's always some concern about strikes or possible layoffs. Do you see why we must be so careful?"

The care has paid off. By the end of 1972, Homes for Black Children had placed more than four hundred children. Where they had started with a backlog of children of all ages waiting for homes, they now have a list of parents waiting for children. Just as in the white community, would-be parents are being asked to consider handicapped children, older children, and those who suffer varying degrees of retardation. There are boys and girls born to heroin-addicted mothers; many are delivered prematurely. The agency is now working to meet these challenges.

The success of an organization such as Homes for Black Children is important in ways that reach out far from Detroit. It attests to the fact that black children are adoptable. It dispels the myth that black families are disinterested in adopting. And it is causing agencies throughout the country to reappraise their thinking and reorganize their programs.

As of October 1973 twenty-five states have enacted legislation to subsidize adoptions in cases where economics prove to be a factor barring a couple from adopting a child. In some of these states the subsidies are available only to foster parents who have held back from making an adoptive commitment because they could not afford to raise the child without outside financial support. In others, moneys are available to all prospective parents who are able to prove need. It is hoped that subsidies will encourage more economically disadvantaged families who can love a child, among them a good number of blacks, to adopt.

That there is no healthy black child up to the age of ten waiting for a home in Detroit is a fact that Sydney Duncan announces with pride. There is some reason to hope this will soon be the case throughout the nation.

Adopting the Older Child

Like most couples who make application to adopt a child, Warren and Harriet Boardman came to the agency in their suburban community outside of Washington, D.C., with a request for an infant. Unlike the majority of couples, however, they were already parents of two biologic children—Christopher, then eight, and four-year-old Susannah.

"The people at the agency pretty much told us, point-blank, that given our ages—Warren was thirty-five and I was just a year younger—and the fact that we were parents to two children, they wouldn't accept our application for an infant. Could we consider an older child," Harriet recalls them asking. "So Warren and I went home and did some real soul-searching."

The Boardmans had lived with the idea of adoption since their newlywed days. Warren was himself raised by foster parents after his biologic parents deserted him in infancy. Though never legally adopted, he assumed the surname of the foster couple who had served as his parents in the best sense of the word. Silently, he also assumed an obligation: to provide a home, someday, for a child who might otherwise remain parentless. "Because

God has been good to me," Warren told Harriet during their courtship, "it's only right that I help somebody else when I'm able." Harriet offered no objection to adopting a child "someday" . . . and that's where the topic was left while the young couple became involved with the business of living—of producing two healthy youngsters and establishing a moderately successful real estate agency in which Harriet still works with her husband, but on a part-time basis. The Boardmans' present home is a sunshine-yellow Colonial that sits on less than an acre in a community of similar, but not carbon copy, estates. This is a neighborhood in which Sunday barbecues are served out-of-doors on redwood tables, the children go to public school, and one out of the two cars in everybody's garage is a secondhand station wagon.

"From time to time," according to Warren, "we would bring up the idea of 'adopting a baby.' Those were our exact words. It took us a year of talking about it before we finally were moved to action. And then the agency people said no. At least that's the way we interpreted their response, even though we were invited to attend a group meeting of couples interested in adoption.

"It was held in the building that housed the adoption agency's offices. There were between thirty and forty couples in the room the night of the meeting. Young couples, older men and women, every kind of person seemed to be there. I remember that there were three or four Jewish couples and they asked what chance there was of their being able to adopt a child. The social worker answered, 'If we get one Jewish child a year, that's a lot!' In our state, adoptions generally are made within religious lines. The requirements can be handled with flexibility, however, where a hard-to-place child is concerned. There were childless men and women at the meeting, single people, and couples who had adopted children previously and were now seeking to enlarge their families. We came away realizing that we had *not* been rejected, but we had been made to face the realities of the adoption situation today. It was up to us to decide whether to pursue adoption."

It didn't help that Harriet's parents, when told what the couple was considering, were not too thrilled with the idea. "If you want more children, why not have your own?" they asked. Warren and Harriet asked themselves that same question. Warren's reply could have been anticipated: he was more interested in helping a homeless child than he was in increasing the size of his family. One of the reasons the Boardmans had waited so long to apply for a child was that they hadn't felt financially able to take on the responsibilities of a larger family before this time in their lives. Harriet was surprised to hear herself respond that she really didn't want to be pregnant again and, while she loved children, she didn't relish the thought of preparing formula and changing diapers. From that awareness, the idea of a post-toddler child became downright attractive.

The Boardmans sounded out their children, too. Since they would be affected by the decision, it was only fitting that they have a say in the matter. Christopher and Susannah were as enthusiastic as their grandparents had been disapproving. (Susannah later came to regret that first, romantic response.)

Warren and Harriet now smile when they look back at how nervous they were when they started out for their first meeting with Mrs. Rogers, the caseworker assigned them after they'd contacted the agency to say yes, they were still interested. ("We didn't know what to say. We didn't have any idea what she would say.") She quickly assured them it was not her intention to sit in judgment, but rather to help the couple learn what kind of child they could parent. What age group could they handle? "Someone younger than our present children," Warren

replied. He and Harriet thought there'd be less chance of
conflict if the new child didn't usurp either Christopher's
or Susannah's place in the family. Mrs. Rogers noted in
her file: maximum age—four.

Would they consider a handicapped youngster?

"Yes, if the handicap is operable." Warren and Harriet
felt they could cope with mild retardation, too, if the little girl (they did favor a female child) could physically
keep up with the children at home.

From the agency point of view, the Boardmans were
excellent candidates. They had a sound marriage and a
genuine liking and respect for children. This was borne
out in the honesty of their dealings with their biologic
children. Social workers also have found it advantageous
for an older child to enter a home where he will find siblings. "Other children in the home can be very good in
helping the new child to adjust," the Boardmans' caseworker later explained. "Their presence dilutes the inten-
sity of all the emotions going on. They show the new boy
or girl the ropes and lay down the family rules. Coming
from the mouths of peers, the rules are more acceptable
to the child. Additionally, many of these children come
to their adoptive homes from institutions or foster homes
in which there are several children. The presence of other
young people makes the strange surroundings in which
the child now finds himself seem less threatening."

There were many meetings to follow—evenings during
which Warren met with Mrs. Rogers, afternoons when
Harriet and she would speak. The Boardmans were asked
such questions as: "If your adoptive daughter would say,
'I liked my other mommy much better than I like you,'
what would be your reaction?" . . . "If your adoptive
daughter and Susannah would have a fight, how would
you handle it?" The separate visits led to joint discussions
at home.

Fifteen months passed in this manner. The agency at

which the Boardmans were registered believes in giving
a lot of casework service in the adoption of an older child
to prepare the new parents and, later, to help them
through the periods of crisis that seem inevitably to follow placement. Then, one day, the Boardmans received
a phone call from Mrs. Rogers. "We have a little girl for
you," she said. "She's three and a half years old. We'd
like to remove her at once from the foster home she's been
in for the last two years. That marriage is breaking up,
with disastrous effect on the children in the home. Will
you take her?"

While adoptive parents of newborns seldom get to
know the child before he or she comes to live with them,
the potential parent of an older child frequently will be
given much helpful information on the youngster, his
strengths and weaknesses (Is he a happy child? outgoing?
a good student?). There may be an exchange of snap-
shots. Often, child and adoptive applicants meet, for all
have to consent to the arrangement. Like a marriage,
adoption of older children often is a mutual consent to
live together. Like a marriage, each side has some giving
in to do. Those who are interested in taking an older child
into their home (any child over a year old has an adjustment problem) must recognize that they will not be able
to mold a formed human being with a past and established tastes and habits into a pattern of life developed
around everything that pleases the adopters.

"When the relationship works, it is tremendously rewarding," commented Barbara Lewis in her former position as director of ARENA, the Adoption Resource Exchange of North America. Miss Lewis continued, "You
experience a developing sense of belonging in a child,
which is wonderful. Children tend to take their parents
for granted, but when you have children who grow to discover that they belong, that someone *really* cares . . . it

takes a long time, but when it comes, it is worth having worked toward."

With a great deal of eagerness, the Boardmans asked Mrs. Rogers, "Is she well?"

"She had a heart murmur as an infant, which held up her being made available for adoption. She seems to have no medical problem at this time. She's been in three foster homes. Incidentally," Mrs. Rogers added, "she's adorable. Her name is Carmel."

Thus, without ever having seen or met the child, the Boardmans said, "We'll take her." That same afternoon, they rushed out and bought twin beds—Carmel was to share a room with Susannah, an arrangement that still obtains—and an Easter bunny for each girl. It was spring.

Two days later, Carmel came home to live. Harriet recalled that first impression: "We opened the door and a little blond girl stood there. She has light blue eyes, almost gray. We're a dark-haired family, yet Carmel and Susannah have the exact same shade of eyes. She had on a sheer pink nylon dress and a tight-fitting winter ski jacket, like the top part of a snowsuit, despite the fact that the day was warm. She reminded me of nothing so much as last year's angel on the Christmas tree.

"For the first six weeks, she behaved like an angel, too," Harriet went on. "I thought I had never seen a better child. She was obedient, never moped about or cried—except when I brushed her teeth. She had *never* brushed her teeth before and her gums bled like crazy. I guess we were a little overzealous about getting her to develop good health habits—bathing regularly, having her hair washed—but she didn't object, so we didn't ease up. That's the only thing we were strict about, however. She seemed like a fragile doll. We handled her with care."

The Boardmans and Carmel were going through the "honeymoon period" that takes place in most older child adoptions—a time of tension (The child is afraid: will they want to keep me?) in which all parties are on their best behavior. Also typical is what took place six weeks later. In Warren's words, "All hell broke loose." Where Carmel had not cried, she never stopped crying. Where she had been obedient, she became contrary. Acquiescence changed to imperiousness, affection to distance. Even the terms "Mommy" and "Daddy," which seemed to have come so easily from Carmel's lips, were replaced by the impersonal "he" and "she."

As Carmel acted out, Susannah suffered most, for it was she who had the most to sacrifice: her own room, her position as youngest and only girl in the family. She'd been queen of the house for five and a half years. Carmel destroyed her toys, messed up her room.

Carmel was testing the entire family and the promises of permanent commitment that had been made to her. Three times in her young life she had been part of a family group. Three times she had been wrenched from surroundings that, while they left much to be desired, had become familiar to her. It is a romantic misconception that all children in foster care wait like prisoners to be released from the custody of the evil wardens (foster parents) to the benevolent human beings who will then adopt them into paradise. So many of these children feel a personal responsibility for abandonment ("I must have done something wrong or they wouldn't have sent me away") and a hesitation to enter a new arrangement, to be twice (or thrice or more) burned. The foster home is at least a known entity. At what point, Carmel was asking by her behavior, would the Boardmans, too, become angry enough to send her away? During the days, she engaged the family members in her struggle. At night, she lay in her room till midnight, wide awake and silent.

Harriet was overcome by exasperation over the daytime child and by compassion for the frail little girl who lay awake, night after night, thinking—what? What mem-

ories of the past visited Carmel in the evening? What fears
for each new day kept her from falling asleep?

"What would you do to Susannah if she was the destructive one?" Mrs. Rogers, the caseworker, asked Harriet and Warren during one of their post-placement conferences.

"I'd give her a swift pat on her backside," Warren replied without hesitation.

"What would you do if Susannah lay awake at night,
seemingly troubled?"

"I'd sit at her bedside and talk with her until she was
calmed," said Harriet.

"Why don't you behave the same way with Carmel?"
suggested Mrs. Rogers. "She's a member of the family,
not a visitor. Let her know you care enough to react."

"Once we stopped handling her with kid gloves, she
stopped being such a pain in the neck," Harriet told me.
"But while we began to treat her more naturally, we
couldn't lose sight of the fact that Carmel had special
needs. For example, I didn't send her to nursery school,
although my two other children had gone to school start-
ing at age three. I felt Carmel had to spend more time
at home, to have me all to herself for part of the day, and
to give me a chance to get to know her better. Mrs. Rogers agreed with that decision. From some clues we've un-
earthed to her past, we think she even may have been
seeking punishment; that may have been the only way she
got any attention in her last foster home."

"During all our early difficulties, only Christopher remained totally protective of his new sister. Then, one day,
fully six months after her arrival, she did something that
annoyed him and he swat out at her instinctively," Warren added. "We knew then that she belonged."

Yet one of the most disturbing—to Harriet—episodes of
Carmel's early months with the family centered around a
punishment. For whatever reason (Harriet can no longer

remember the cause), Carmel had misbehaved and Harriet had punished her by ordering the little girl to sit in a chair in the kitchen while she went about her work. So unaccustomed was Harriet to having a child at home during school hours, she simply forgot about Carmel. One and a half hours later, she remembered the little girl. "Oh my God," she reacted. "Where's Carmel?" And there the child sat, motionless, in that kitchen chair. Harriet was horrified by her own forgetfulness and insensitivity. Even more, she wondered, "What little child is so cowed that she will sit still for so long, afraid to move? What past experience has made her so frightened?"

This lack of knowledge of the past is disturbing to many who adopt older children. Mrs. Eligia Lorenti, senior supervisor at the Adoption Service of Westchester, a small agency that now finds almost half its case load comprised of children past the age of one, tries to prepare her parents to deal with the problems of helping a child to really integrate all the experiences he's been through, without specific knowledge of those experiences. "It is the adoptive parents' job to try to elicit that history and help the youngsters come to grips with it," she explains. "That is often a difficult, and painful, process."

Kathryn Donley, director of Michigan's Spaulding for Children, an agency established in 1968 with the specific task of placing children with special needs, warns those interested in older child adoption of the multitude of problems they may have to face. Mrs. Donley asks parents to consider:

"What do you do when the child has a phobic fear of dogs, and you don't know where the fear comes from?

"What do you do when you feel you can cope with bed-wetting and the child has wet the bed ten nights in a row and you're out of clean sheets and you're ready to tear your hair out?

"What do you do when you find medical or psychological problems turn out to be greater than you'd been led to expect?

"What do you do when your child gets into a fight with the neighbor's boy—and yours is newly adopted?

"What do you do when your biologic child hits your adopted child and says, 'Go back where you came from. I'm sick of you.'?

"What do you do when you ask how many homes the child's been in and the social worker answers, 'Maybe four . . . or ten.'?

"What do you do when love alone won't do it?

"What you do"—and here she answers her own questions—"is decide that love, and commitment, will have to do it."

"What do you do," adds Harriet Boardman, "when your adopted child looks through the blue and pink vinyl-covered baby books you've compiled with records of your older children's achievements and asks, 'Mommy, when did I start to walk? At what age did I begin to talk? What were my first baby words?' That used to upset me terribly, both because I didn't have the answers for Carmel and because I had missed being a witness to those important firsts. What I did was admit my lack of knowledge and start a special book beginning with the important facts of Carmel's life as we knew them: the day she came to our house; the first time she rode a tricycle; the morning she entered kindergarten."

Harriet and Warren's interest in Carmel's past goes beyond curiosity about the child's lineage. She has been in her new home two years now, and her parents have not discovered why she lay awake at night. They *have* learned there were times when she was tied to a chair seat, hence her fear to budge when Harriet punished her in a similar manner. Needless to say, that punishment has never been used since. Harriet faults the agency she and Warren dealt with on only one point—the reluctance of its employees to divulge any information about Carmel other than the age of her parents, both seventeen at the time of her birth, and the state in which she was born. "I would have liked to have known about any family talents so I could encourage them in the child. I would have liked more information on Carmel's heritage so I could pass it along to her when she questons her identity in later years," Harriet says.

This lack of knowledge of events in a child's past causes, at the least, some uncomfortable moments for all who adopt older children. One typical incident, having to do with health history, is cited in Alfred Kadushin's interesting work, *Adopting Older Children,* a study of ninety-one families who adopted children five and older at the time of placement. Dr. Kadushin quotes the adoptive mother of an older daughter: "We still have to ask her [the daughter] when somebody says, 'Did your daughter have measles or something, so that you'd better not let her in,' so I have to say, 'L——, do you remember having them?' Because I don't know."

Many older children remember a great deal about their past, but will not confide those recollections—some experiences being either too painful or too precious to relate. Nine-year-old Patrick Vega now is able to explain why he always takes some extra food from the table "for later" even though he has been assured he may snack when hungry. For at least a year, he did not confess that he'd been denied second helpings in his foster home. Interestingly, the Boardmans and several other parents interviewed had also told me about a constant craving for food by the newly adopted child, which seemed to exist at all age levels and even in those cases where the youngsters were obviously well nourished, as was Patrick. It seems that the child lives for some time after placement with a fear that this new living arrangement will be a temporary one, despite assurances to the contrary. Symbolically, he can never be certain of where his next meal will come from. He stores up today for a possible abandonment tomorrow.

Like Carmel Boardman, Patrick Vega lies awake for long periods each night, remembering. He is encouraged to speak of this by his parents when I visit with the family.

"What do you think about at night?" I ask.

"You know, lots of things," he stammers.

"It's all right, Patrick. We won't be upset by what you say," he is told by his doting parents. Their only child after years of wanting a large family, which they sadly learned they could not conceive, Patrick is very special to them. He knows it, therefore is solicitous of their feelings.

"Well, I think about lots of things. I think about what it's like here, and I think about my other home, the one before this one."

"Did you like it there?" I ask.

"Yes. I miss the warm weather—we could always go fishing—but I like to play in the snow here." Patrick spent the first seven years of his life with one foster family, down South, and now makes his home in the northern section of the country.

"And what else do you think about?"

He is hesitant. His parents cue him: "We're sure you miss the other children who lived with Aunt Betty and Uncle Lou [his foster parents; Rachel and Nick have taken over the roles and titles of Mom and Dad]. After all, they were your friends."

"My *friends?* They're my brothers." For a moment, he is sure. "Yes, I think about them. I miss them."

"Of course you do," Rachel Vega says. She tousles Pat's

fine red hair, gives him a quick kiss which he returns un-self-consciously—unusual, I think, for a boy child of nine.

"What do you like best about your new house?" I ask.

"Mom's cooking." The answer comes easily. "And not sharing a bed." Pat shows the visitor his room. It is a typical blue boy's bedroom containing lots of sports equipment: a basketball for the hoop over the garage, a bowling ball, ice skates, a football helmet.

"Do you like sports?"

"My dad's a great skater," says Pat.

He is obviously relieved to be told he can join the neighborhood children whose voices are quite audible through the screen door leading from the Vegas' small backyard to their cozy yellow kitchen, where we sat and recalled how Patrick had come to live with the folks who are now his own.

The Vegas' story, which differs from that of the Boardmans, is similar to the history of many older, childless couples who come to adopt older, parentless youngsters. When they were married, at age twenty-nine and thirty-one (a second marriage for Rachel, whose childhood romance failed the test of time), Rachel and Nick agreed they wanted a large family, the sooner the better. Their plans were not fulfilled. Medical tests indicated the difficulty lay with Rachel, who was put on a program of fertility pills. "We were even elated at the possibility of multiple births which I'd heard sometimes resulted from taking the pills," Rachel recalled. "That meant more children more quickly." When the pills proved ineffective, Rachel underwent major surgery, although her doctor only held out as "possible" a result that would enable her to become pregnant. Finally came the day when he told her, frankly, "It seems unlikely that you and Nick will become parents. Perhaps you ought to consider adoption."

They had never been against the idea of adopting a child, although Rachel was fearful of being rejected by an agency because of her earlier divorce. "We were really so dumb about the whole business of adoption," she now says, thinking back to the morning when she and Nick drove up to the city-run agency, so nervous that, in Nick's words, "It took us ten minutes just to get out of the car."

"The first thing I remember doing was blurting out the fact that I was divorced," Rachel says. "Instead of condemning me, the lady behind the desk reassured me. She asked how long Nick and I had been married. I said, 'Seven years.' The important consideration in placing a child, she explained, was what kind of home he was going into. While that might exclude someone who had a history of mate-swapping, it certainly left room for that person who had made a mistake in her past but whose present life seemed secure."

"After we relaxed," said Nick, and from this time on he took over most of the conversation, "we expressed our desires and our needs. We never felt we were pushed toward a child we couldn't handle. This was going to be our first child, and we wanted a healthy one, boy or girl; sex didn't matter. Because the picture of a child that we held in our minds was of a baby, we asked for an infant.

"One day, our caseworker phoned and asked, 'Would you consider an older child? A southern agency has sent us information on a seven-year-old boy in foster care who is now available for adoption.'

"I told Rachel what was said, and the two of us looked at one another in amazement. 'You mean,' we asked, 'if we say that we want him, we can get him?' She said yes. 'My God, *yes*,' we shouted."

The Vegas quickly phoned all their friends and relatives, who joined them in a celebration that lasted all weekend.

The following Monday, the social worker dropped by with a picture of Patrick. It is now worn from handling. In it, Pat looks much the same as when I was introduced to him, the noticeable difference being the two large front teeth that have grown in to fill the empty space created by the loss of his baby teeth. The dimple in his left cheek is more evident in person. The Vegas were asked to take pictures of themselves—they are a tall couple: Nick gives an immediate impression of controlled physical strength; Rachel looks like the best advertisement for her own good cooking—and of their house, car, and immediate neighborhood. These were sent, air mail, to Patrick.

Then Nick and Rachel flew south to meet Pat. At the agency's suggestion, they stayed at a motel that had a housekeeping unit as part of the accommodations, so that any time they spent with Pat during this trial period would approximate normal life as much as possible. Rachel was to prepare lunch while Nick and Pat spent some social time together. In many states, the older child can decide if he wants to go with the adults who have been selected as his potential parents. Several children (generally those already into their teens) have opted to remain in foster care rather than take their chances with new authority figures in their lives. Pat cried when he learned he might be adopted. He didn't want to leave his foster home nor did he understand why the other boys remained behind while he was being sent away. (The fact Pat can live with is that his Aunt Betty and Uncle Lou were older people who had raised their own children and could not assume the burden of a permanent second family. He has never been told they favored one of the three boys and have initiated procedures to adopt that child, two years Pat's senior, which is another reason it was deemed advisable to remove Pat from their home.)

The agency worker recalls that Patrick's impression after his initial visit to Nick and Rachel had to do with Nick's size. "He's big," Patrick commented. Uncle Lou was a small man and Patrick was the smallest of the three boys in the home. Rachel recalls turning to Nick and saying, "Oh, God, I don't know if I like him. Maybe we're making a big mistake." She lay awake all night, dreading the boy's next visit, which took place the following morning.

Patrick was brought to the motel by the southern agency's caseworker. Then he, Nick, and Rachel went for a drive. Both the silences and the conversation were awkward. How did Patrick like school? Were there many children in the immediate neighborhood of the Vegas' house? Did Patrick like to build things? Did the Vegas own a color TV? Could Patrick direct them to the local park? "Dad," Patrick blurted out, "when we get back to the motel, can I go for a swim in the pool?"

From that moment on, the adoption procedure was a formality to be overcome. Rachel and Nick had steeled themselves to the possibility of two or three visits south before they won the boy over. At the end of this first week, he announced that he wanted to go back home— to his own home—with them.

The three of them came north by plane, again at the suggestion of the caseworker who felt that a long automobile journey would be physically and emotionally taxing, and Patrick immediately felt at home in his new surroundings. Everything looked just like the photographs he'd been sent.

He did not, for some time, stray three feet from his mother's side except to go to school, where his "honeymoon" manners were obvious even to his teachers. As his homeroom teacher told Rachel, who was herself unaccustomed to the new world of schools and parent-teacher conferences, "He's overgood."

Rachel knew what the teacher meant. "I couldn't wait for the day when Patrick would say, 'No!'" she recalls. "I kept asking him to go outside and play with other children. He was reluctant to leave me. No matter what he was involved in, every few minutes he'd come and check on my whereabouts, kiss me, and go back to whatever he was doing."

"It's funny how you suddenly begin to notice children all around you," Nick says. "Here we were, two people who got up and went to work and went out in the evening because there was nothing to keep us at home. There are a lot of kids in the neighborhood, but I'd never paid them any attention. Suddenly, I'd be driving home from my job at the airport [Nick is involved with aspects of airport security] and I'd really look at the kids playing ball in the street and think, 'This one might be a good age for Patrick,' or 'That one looks a little too old.'

"But it took a long time before he'd go out and play with any of the children. 'Call up a friend from school,' we'd suggest, 'and invite him over.' Patrick didn't know what it was like to make a phone call; he'd never spoken on the telephone except to answer it when his foster mother asked him to, and he'd never placed a call to anyone in his life. We eventually had to force him to go out and play. Now, we have to holler to get him to come in for dinner.

"After Patrick came to live with us, I spent all day at work waiting to go home to my kid—and when I got there, he spent all of his time with Rachel. He'd started out as my pal, and now I didn't seem to count at all." The couple had reversed their roles and their reactions. Now Rachel was Pat's companion and confidante. "She kept telling me how much she loved the boy," says Nick, "and I didn't yet. Not the kind of love she meant. One day, I walked out into the backyard and found myself pouting because Patrick loved Rachel more than he did me. What I mean to say is, we all had some adjustments to make."

One of the mistakes the Vegas own up to is trying to give Patrick too much too soon. Nick ran out and bought

him a three-speed bicycle with hand brakes when the
boy couldn't pedal a simpler model. Yet Patrick didn't
want to disappoint his new father by telling him the bike
was *too* special, so he kept attempting to ride the bicycle
in his father's presence, left it in the garage during the
week. It wasn't until a year later that the father could
admit his son wasn't ready for so splendid a gift, recommended that it be sold and the money used to purchase a
less costly, less contrived bike. His son agreed, relieved.

Much of the tension which Patrick was unable to ver-
balize found release through physical means. He was in-
continent, often wetting his pants at school and at home,
out-of-doors or in. Nick and Rachel had tried several suc-
cessive approaches to the problem: largely understanding
and promises of reward if Patrick would learn to go to the
bathroom before he'd leave the house. Nothing worked.
One day, Rachel found herself at wit's end when Patrick
urinated through his clothing in the aisle of a department store minutes after his mother had asked him
if he wanted to pay a visit to the boy's room. "When,"
Rachel asked her caseworker in the opening minutes of
their next meeting, "can I start applying some discipline
to this child?"

"Right now," was the answer.

More than discipline, time and security have solved
that problem.

Obviously at home in his blue room, Patrick speaks
less and less of Aunt Betty and Uncle Lou as time goes
on. Now studying heredity in school, he has shifted his
interest to queries about his biologic mother. "Where did
she come from?" he asks.

"She was of Irish ancestry," he is told.

"Who was my father?"

"He was a male Caucasian. That's all we know."

"What did he look like?"

"He must have been very handsome," Rachel tells her son, "because you're such a good-looking boy."

Patrick comes in from play. As I gather my notes, preparing to say good-by to the family, he runs into his room and brings me a picture of the two boys who lived with him in his foster home. "These are my brothers," he says. I remark that they're handsome boys, which is indeed the case, and Patrick seems pleased, wanting me to approve of his past as I now seem to delight in his present. Patrick must reconcile the two, plus face up to the fact of his original abandonment, if he is to grow to well-adjusted manhood.

The odds are good that he will succeed. This point is well made in Kadushin's *Adopting Older Children*. "The most significant general, over-all conclusion of the study is that older children can be placed for adoption with expectation that the placement will work out to the satisfaction of the adoptive parents," Kadushin wrote in his chapter on "The Reversibility of Trauma." His most surprising finding is that the level of expectation of satisfying outcome is only slightly lower than that which might be anticipated in adoptive placement of infants.

Kadushin further commented, "The general conclusion is unexpected and raises a question of considerable interest. . . . The early lives of these children, who spent their most impressionable years under conditions of poverty, inadequately housed, with alcoholic, promiscuous parents who frequently neglected them, sometimes abused them, and only rarely offered them the loving care prerequisite to wholesome emotional development make it difficult to explain the generally favorable outcome of these placements."

Part of the explanation is provided in a discussion of the "special advantages" of older child adoption as related by the adoptive parents. Kadushin reports, "Many, coming as they did to adoptive parenthood relatively late in life, felt that the older child was the more appropriate choice for them. A preference for infants, expressed during the study period, is subject to modification as a result of the adoptive experience itself. Some who came expressing desire for an infant were able to accept the idea of adopting an older child at the end of the study period. Some who adopted the older child with some ambivalence became, as a result of the adoptive experience, strongly positive in their attitude about the desirability of older children for older parents because of the age spread."

This certainly proved to be the case in the Vega household. "After we asked for a baby—because that seemed right for a first child," Nick explains, "Rachel and I began to face reality. We were in our late thirties. If we'd been successful when we first tried to conceive, that baby would have been six or seven years old by the time we made application to adopt. Even then, we wouldn't have been considered young parents. All of our friends were done with child-bearing. It made sense for us to be parents to an older child."

The Vegas have made application to adopt a second child—not a baby. "I don't think I could handle an infant now, or chase after a toddler," says Rachel. "Our only request was that the child, boy or girl, be younger than Pat, so he doesn't lose his special place in our family."

▲ Adults interviewed by Kadushin also mentioned as advantageous the fact that the adopted older child fits in with the ages of children in the parents' peer group, which they found made for better adjustment for both. The youngster is capable of participating in many of the family activities and is, consequently, more stimulating and interesting to the parents, more responsible, more appreciative.

Kadushin continues, "While the older child requires more discipline, since he is more active and more capable of mischief, he is also easier to discipline; as one parent said, 'You can explain to them why they can't do certain things, and you can reason with them . . . they are talkable children.'"

The nontalkable child who is, nevertheless, past infant stage can be more exasperating than the child who has a longer, perhaps more trauma-filled past but who is able to talk out his experiences. "You can't imagine what it's like," one Midwestern mother told me, "to have a one-and-a-half-year-old little girl cry with terror every time you approach her, to convulse when you reach out to soothe her, and you don't know what happened in her past to so frighten her nor how to deal with it." In this family's case, the little girl was returned to her foster home, where she relaxed in surroundings that were familiar to her. The caseworker now is encouraging that family to take steps to adopt the child.

Echoes of that experience were heard in conversations with the Boardmans, who had adopted Carmel at age three and a half. "You know the old saying, 'We wouldn't take a million for her, but I wouldn't give you two cents for a duplicate,'" said Harriet Boardman, "well, that's about the way Warren and I feel about Carmel. We're secure in our love for her, and can't imagine our home without her, but—looking back—we think three and a half is a difficult age for adoption. It's a deceptive age. The child can talk, so you think she can explain things to you. You also fall into the trap of believing she understands what you're saying to her. She nods and gets the words all right, but not really what you're trying to get across. If we adopt again, I'd like a child, probably a boy, who has passed his fifth birthday."

There are such children available. Although one adoption worker I spoke with referred to any child older than two as "a geriatric loser on the adoption circuit," there is evidence of an increase in adoption of younger "older children." According to Mrs. Loyce Bynum, associate

director of adoptions at New York's Spence-Chapin
agency, "We're beginning to define older as 'older and
older.' There was a time when older was eighteen months.
Now it may be school age: five or six years."

A corollary advantage of adopting the "older older
child," cited in the Kadushin study, is that parents receive
the participation and assistance of the adoptive child in
ensuring the success of the adoption. The older child
"adopts" the family as well as being adopted *by* the family. He is a child who wants to be adopted.

The recurrent difficulties mentioned by parents during
the Kadushin interviews suggest some of the particular
disadvantages in adopting an older child: "Sixty per
cent of the parents mentioned that the child had been
molded by others during an earlier period in his life, and
they were faced with the problem of changing patterns of
behavior to which the child had become habituated."
Since the children generally were adopted upward, coming from lower-class backgrounds to middle-class adoptive homes, they had to adjust to different norms, habits,
diet. Many were unaccustomed to sitting down to dinner
with a family. (Some youngsters I spoke with recalled
having been served separately from their foster families,
with children's menus notably inferior to what the adults
were given to eat.)

Kadushin's findings underline this: "The meals pre-
ferred by these children featured hot dogs, hamburgers,
beans and Cokes. What could be cooked quickly, or what
came out of a can, were apt to be familiar. Green vegetables and salads were likely to be rejected because they
were unfamiliar. Once again, these are differences between a lower-class diet and a middle-class diet."

Adoptive parents I interviewed complained about the
excessive amounts of time the children spent in front of
the television set—which may indicate that it was used as

a baby sitter in previous residences or that more stimulating activities weren't offered to the children.

Fifty per cent of Kadushin's interviewees cited as disadvantageous the fact that "such children, having lived under stressful circumstances, come to adoption with emotional difficulty; 45 per cent noted that they found it hard to understand the child, since one has only limited knowledge of his previous life and experience; 29 per cent of the families expressed some disappointment at having missed the joys and pleasures of growing with the child from his early infancy; and 24 per cent felt anxious about some competition with the other parental figures the child had known and loved."

Addressing himself to this final point, Nick Vega says, "Rachel and I think about the future often. We know that Patrick will have memories of his foster home. With the years, he will probably create a more romantic picture of that home because we will be his reality—which means that while we love him, we will also have to discipline him. We've even talked about how we would feel if he grows up and rejects us, going south to reunite with his foster brothers if they do manage to keep in touch. We don't think that's likely to happen, but we've faced the possibility. Here's how we look at it: nobody has any guarantees about the future. We keep reading about teen-agers who run away from their homes—and they aren't necessarily adopted children. One thing we do know. Whatever Patrick does in the years to come, we will have had *these* years with him. They're a lot happier and more fulfilling than the years that came before."

✗ Adopting the Handicapped Child

A birth-defect baby, "Cindy" was born without arms or legs, yet her caseworker's first thought, upon being sent a picture of this homeless child, was, "What a beautiful face." The reactions of this woman's co-workers to the same photograph were, "Oh how awful" and "What a terrible pity." Because this first worker looked upon ✗ Cindy as a person, including the child's handicap but not to the exclusion of the beautiful face, she was able to set about finding a permanent home for the infant. She telephoned a family who had previously adopted a child—a healthy older boy—from the agency and told the members about this lovely girl who badly needed a home.

Cindy's new mother tells the story from there: "After we were called, we held a family conference. We agreed that we wanted a little girl and that we'd take the one who needed us most. Our fear with Cindy was that we wouldn't be financially able to provide the care she needed. When we were told help was available for us through our state's Crippled Children's Commission, we began to call Cindy our baby. While we waited, that's about all we talked about. When she finally arrived, everyone was well prepared and relaxed about her handicap.

Our son treats her like she's normal and enjoys helping to care for her.

"Cindy is very easy to care for. It doesn't take long to put her limbs on her. Then we spend about fifteen minutes helping her walk. After that, she stands alone for fifteen minutes. She's pretty, smart, and independent, trying something new every day and enjoying the applause when she finishes. This is a very rewarding experience for all of us. If we give her love and care (physical and emotional) she'll do okay when she's older. I have no doubts. She is really going somewhere!

"We're all happy she's ours."

While such placements happen infrequently, even today, more professionals in the adoption field are actively seeking homes for their severely handicapped youngsters, those previously consigned to institutions or long-range foster care because they were judged "unadoptable." In a 1962 issue of the government-sponsored magazine *Children*, Missouri child welfare supervisor Alice Hornecker asked, "Does the social work principle, 'Every child has a right to a home and a family that loves and wants him for himself,' include the severely handicapped or mentally defective child?" The question was rhetorical, yet little effort was being expended to seek adoptive homes for these children with special needs. There were healthy babies to be placed. Few couples came forward on their own to accept the challenge of the handicapped or to reap the rewards of raising such youngsters.

Kathryn Donley of Michigan's Spaulding for Children attributes the increase in placements of children like Cindy and those with less serious handicaps to two factors: (a) the dearth of healthy white babies, which has caused agency people to take a look at the other children in their files; (b) pressure by parents' groups to find a home for every waiting child.

"We can't pat ourselves on the back because we now

have statistics to show for our placement of these 'available' children," Mrs. Donley told a group of her fellow professionals recently. "We all know that too many of us have still to get rid of our own hang-ups about physical deformities and retardation. The *parents* are the key to the success of this program. *They're* the ones who have been in the forefront of this new trend in adoption. *They've* been the agitators for change. The profession of social work will never change from within; it's filled with conservatives. But it will move if spurred by outside forces."

❋ Kay Donley speaks from experience. Spaulding was established as a direct result of a seminar, *Frontiers in Adoption,* which determined that hard-to-place children were not receiving adequate attention and service to make an appreciable dent in their rapidly increasing numbers. The seminar itself came about largely through the efforts of an adoptive couple, Peter and Joyce Forsythe, founders of a vigorous parent organization, Michigan's Council on Adoptable Children.

❋ "Initially, we demonstrated our ability to find adoptive homes for 'problem' children by waiving fees to agencies that referred some of their children to us, which encouraged them to enlist our help," Kay Donley explains. "Now we charge them a five hundred dollar purchase-of-service fee for each child in their custody whom we place, which is still under the cost to them had they handled the entire adoption. There is no cost to any parent with whom we place a child. I feel very strongly about this. I see adoption as a service to a child, to find him a home, and feel that a fee system is detrimental to creating more homes. It keeps families of modest means, who could otherwise care for and love a child, from approaching agencies that have the children. The cost of adoption should always be underwritten by the government—no matter how you look at it, it's a cheaper program than any other form of custodial care and ultimately saves the government money.

"The cost of medical treatment should be covered by existing institutions, too," Donley believes. "Social workers have a responsibility to learn about what federal and local funding exists to help the handicapped, and to pass this information on to those who might be encouraged to adopt youngsters whose special needs are likely to incur special expense. If there are no subsidies in their cities or states, agency personnel ought to lead a lobby to agitate for subsidy legislation." It is this kind of action-oriented thinking that has enabled Spaulding to place more than a hundred nearly forgotten children. "When we founded Spaulding, we thought we were in the vanguard of something," says its director. "We found instead that we were in the midst of a movement going on all over the country."

At about the same time as the Frontiers in Adoption seminar was convened, the Child Welfare League of America set up the Adoption Resource Exchange of North America (ARENA), a central clearinghouse to unite available children with willing families across the continent. (Today, forty-two states have their own adoption exchanges, some more formal than others, established to permit agencies to trade information on available children and waiting homes; ARENA generally is consulted when local attempts fail.) While the exchanges have set no guidelines for children registered with them—theoretically, they could place healthy white infants with adoptive parents—as a practical matter their services are purchased only for those children that a local agency has difficulty placing, i.e. older and handicapped youngsters.

ARENA's successes speak eloquently for the importance of this kind of exchange. The 1972 report on its fifth year of operation cited agencies from all fifty states, the District of Columbia, Puerto Rico, Virgin Islands, and seven of the Canadian provinces participating in

✳ARENA. There were 243 children placed for adoption, bringing the total number of placements since the beginning of ARENA to 989. Twenty-eight of these children were limited intellectually; twenty-three had correctable physical handicaps, thirty-seven non-correctable. The kinds of handicap represented in the non-correctable category include heart defects, albinism, hydrocephalus, severe asthma, neurological dysfunctions and learning disabilities. In addition, five deaf, four blind and two dwarf children were placed. The placement of one of these dwarf children, who was born in Illinois, with a dwarf family in Australia illustrates the importance of a far-reaching exchange. In this situation, Barbara Lewis, then director of ARENA, worked with Little People of America, an organization whose membership is made up of dwarfed persons and their families. These people are greatly concerned with the plight of dwarf children, whom they dub "little littles," for they know such youngsters too often are mislabeled retarded because of their slower rate of development (which is normal for a dwarf child) and because of physical characteristics such as the head being large in proportion to the rest of the body—common in certain cases of dwarfism and of retardation—and that these children are then categorized as unadoptable. Little People of America is only one of many special interest groups that offer proof of the existence of a home for each child with special needs. The task that remains for social workers is to locate—or create—that home.

ARENA brought Jodi, a little redhead born with a cleft lip and cleft palate, from the Midwest to the attention of an agency in the East and, eventually, to the home of Naomi and Gary Fields. Since theirs is a fairly typical case of a family that did not seek a handicapped child at the outset, let us follow the story of this adoption.

When Naomi and Gary finally decided to implement their prenuptial plan to create a family of two biological and two adopted children, they were one child ahead on their biological schedule. Their household now held Rhonda, Jared, and Noah. An article in their local newspaper on "unadoptable children" made them recall their early ambition. Since in this account "unadoptable" was defined as "interracial," the Fields concluded they would provide a home for an interracial child. It was that simple. Naomi's inquiry at the local office of her state's adoption service resulted in an invitation to attend a group meeting for people interested in adopting.

At the meeting, the need for homes for black and interracial youngsters was stressed. The Fields were given an application for adoption, which they mailed in the following week. When the caseworker assigned to them in follow-up to their application changed two appointments (for which Gary, a biology instructor at a local high school, had arranged to be present) in a slipshod manner, the Fields became angered and discouraged.

While waiting in line before a check-out counter in her local supermarket, Naomi struck up a conversation with the white adoptive mother of a black child, who was seated in her shopping cart, and told of her frustrations in trying to arrange a similar adoption. This woman suggested the agency she had worked with, a smaller organization in a neighboring city of the same state in which the Fields family makes its home.

Here Naomi and Gary found not only an interested caseworker but one who acted as "a stimulus for growth," according to Naomi, "spurring us to face ourselves honestly and to live up to what we could expect from ourselves." (Again and again interviewees impressed me with this fact: if you run into difficulties as you wander the adoption maze, the fault may not lie in your sense of direction but in your guide. Do not hesitate to change workers—even agencies—if you feel that, despite your best efforts, you're not moving forward.)

What the worker sensed, and Gary and Naomi later
came to acknowledge, was that they did not see themselves as parents to a child of another race. Nor did they
believe their three children could easily accept a black
brother or sister. The Fields were thinking of a black
child in the same terms as they welcomed the black boy
who came to spend several weeks with them in their suburban community each summer under the auspices of a
church-sponsored fresh-air program. He was a very nice
boy and the entire family had grown fond of him. Could
they call this child of another race "son"?

When the honest response turned out to be "No," they
began to fear adoption might not be for them and were
dismayed. Tentatively, Naomi (who was trained as a
nurse) asked her worker about handicapped children.
Gary vacillated on this. The worker's reply was, "Go home
and pick out a handicap; then figure out how you would
be able to handle it."

Naomi made this her project. She read about a child
who was born without a hand, and felt that this would be
manageable. Next, she called the charitable agencies in
her community to learn what money was available to
help families pay for braces, prosthesis, possible operations. She and Gary knew they could not afford heavy
medical bills. The answers they met with were discouraging (their state did not have a medical subsidy program; many do) until they reached the Easter Seals people, who were extremely helpful.

"When we came into the agency with all the information we'd gathered, our caseworker knew we were serious
and began our interviews and home study," Gary reported.

Their worker underlined this. "It is very important for
anyone who seeks to help a child needing special care to
find out everything about services in the community. For
example, you don't do much good for a retarded child if

you have him placed in your home and then discover there are no classes for slow learners in your community, so that the child is denied a good education which will do much to help him function in a world that moves quickly. You must then be willing to move to a neighborhood where such a program does exist or face up to the fact that a different child will do better with you," she explained. When the Fields first approached the agency, they were filled with the romance of adopting. As they researched the possibilities that lay before them, they made the important transition to reality.

They began to work seriously with their caseworker in May. By August, Gary and Naomi had agreed on a possible variety of manageable handicap. Equally important, they'd decided there were some that were beyond their capabilities. Among the latter were cerebral palsy, mongolism, and emotional disturbances. It was important that their child be mobile and intelligent. Yes, a blind or deaf youngster could fit these qualifications.

Naomi was out raking the first of the fall's tumbling leaves when she was called to the phone. It was the caseworker. She had received the current ARENA listings. "There is a little girl not yet a year old, out West. She has a cleft lip and cleft palate. What do you think?"

Naomi remembers: "I felt like jumping for joy and, at the same time, I was a bit let down. Here I'd been keyed up for a major thing, and now I could have a child with an operable disability. 'How soon can we see her?' I asked."

Within two weeks, Naomi and Gary drove out West in a camper-trailer, for they were required to meet Jodi at the offices of the agency that had custody of the child. Naomi describes that visit: "We walked into the room where Jodi was playing with a Raggedy Ann doll. Her hair was red like Raggedy's—no, a bit lighter—and she was seated on the floor. She turned and I was startled—not by

how terrible she looked, but because she didn't look as
bad as I'd anticipated. Her palate was open on the inside, but she'd already undergone surgery to close her lip.
I was grateful for that. I knew that children born with
this abnormality look awful before the lip is closed. Her
nose was flat because of the cleft and her eyes . . . well,
we didn't really notice her eyes until later.

"I went over to her, to pick her up, and she stood up
and ran straight to Gary. That was a blow because I expected a baby and here she was walking. We didn't know
what to do with her, so we took her for a ride and she
slept in my arms in the car."

Jodi had spent the first months of her life in an excellent foster home. Her foster mother had provided her
adoptive family with a detailed list of instructions for her
care. The first instructions had to do with feeding the
baby. Since Jodi's palate was open, food kept coming out
of her nose. "She has to be fed a lot so that she'll keep
down some of the food," the note read. "You have to let
her drink slowly from a cup because she cannot drink
very quickly."

Gary held Jodi while Naomi fed her. "I was afraid I
wouldn't be able to feed her," Naomi says. "I didn't experience revulsion—Gary was marvelous—but I was tenta-
tive. As I fed Jodi and food dribbled from her nose, I kept
wiping it up. Later, I stopped that foolishness. It gets so
that you kind of develop a technique to avoid spillage.
Gary and I were on relatively comfortable ground so long
as we were busied with tending to Jodi's physical needs.
It was while she slept that we were tense. You see, we
felt that we should love her completely—she was, after all,
going to be our daughter—but we didn't. We also were
concerned about her eyes. They had a slanted shape, pe-
culiar to mongolism, and we feared she might be retarded. Later, we raised this doubt and were assured
that a chromosome study, used to diagnose mongolism,

had been done on Jodi and the results were negative. And so we took Jodi home.

"We had no problems with our children at home—they're great—but Gary and I continued to be concerned about not loving her. Our caseworker told us not to worry. 'It takes time to fall in love' is the way she put it. I can't tell you when that time came—it only took a few months —but now she's mine."

Naomi knows that her change in attitude toward Jodi can be traced through her own behavior during each of the two operations Jodi has undergone in the more than two years she has been a Fields daughter. Following the operation to close her lip (done when Jodi was three months old), the little girl underwent difficult surgery to close her palate. A soft palate was formed. Jodi spent eight days in the hospital, during which she was fed intravenously for much of the time. The first few postoperative days, Jodi was in an oxygen tent. Naomi, a former nurse, took all this objectively. It had to be done.

The next operation, to create a cupid's bow above Jodi's upper lip, was largely cosmetic and relatively minor. Nevertheless, Naomi recalls, "I was *sick*. This was no longer a medical case—*it was Jodi!*"

For the first of the two operations, Jodi continued to be covered by the Medicaid program of the state in which she was born. The expense of the second was completely covered by Blue Cross. Jodi may require two more palate operations and have plastic surgery done to improve the appearance of her nose, which has a crooked nostril (this had to be pointed out to me; it is not a glaring defect but is something that might bother a teen-age girl). She will need orthodontics. The cost of this is not covered by any medical plan the Fields know of, but there's an orthodontist in town who is also an adoptive parent and he has been generous indeed, philanthropic—in his work with adopted children referred to him by the agency. Gary is confident that he will be able to rely on his health insurance program to cover future medical expenses. "We've tested them and they've come through. We're delighted," he says. Jodi now is taken for speech therapy twice a week. The cost at the clinic she attends is $30 a year. Incidentally, the adoption agency waived their customary fee when they learned it would be difficult for Naomi and Gary to make the payment.

It was not easy for this couple to decide to adopt a handicapped child; they were not a man and wife filled with a sense of mission. Their life was full. Gary enjoys his work. He and Naomi are active in their church. In their spare time, they tend to become involved in do-it-yourself projects. This year Naomi made all the menfolk in her family ski jackets. Gary built an aquarium into the wall of the boys' bedroom and Rhonda executed a fairly professional mural in her own bedroom.

The family members enjoy one another. They are particularly saddened by the fact that Naomi's father will have little to do with Jodi. A man who takes great pride in "good stock," he is opposed to the very idea of allowing "a stranger's blood" into the family. For some time he would not enter Naomi and Gary's home; then his longing to see his grandchildren grew to be too much for him. Because Jodi was young, he was allowed to visit, but when Jodi ran to him and hugged his leg in a spontaneous gesture, he pulled back, repulsed. Naomi doubts he will be able to overcome this reaction.

"I look at Jodi and I don't see that she's not pretty," says Naomi. Nor does the visitor. The impression one comes away with is of a bubbly little girl with tousled red hair who is quick to smile and to ask questions and to kiss. Every child in a home brings problems. Like every child, Jodi also contributes a special kind of joy.

✳ Those who are able to recognize the potential for joy are those who can consider adopting the handicapped.

Some parents are uniquely capable of dealing with a specific disability—a teacher of the blind who adopts a blind daughter, dwarf parents for a "little little," the mother and father of a mongoloid son, now into his teen years, who feel their experience in raising him makes them able to love and teach a second child who is similarly afflicted. In other cases, the adoption agency must help potential adopters to *understand* the disability, to *accept* it, and eventually to *parent* the child with special needs.

❋ Talking with parents who have successfully coped with a child's need is most helpful. Many couples who seek to adopt a child today are told of the availability of large numbers of children who are retarded—an adjective that seems to carry with it an indictment so strong that adoption workers frequently tend to refer to these youngsters as "slow learners" or "underachievers." In 70 per cent of these cases, these euphemisms are quite accurate, for the children who are mildly retarded are educable youngsters.

❋A speaker at a meeting of an organization named Mothers of Mongoloids told an audience assembled at an adoption conference, "If you can be parents to children who will never go to college but who will grow, *with your help*, to be able to earn an honest living—as cafeteria workers or assembly line people—you can consider adopting these children." Another 25 per cent are moderately retarded children who will need special training and guidance. "If you will be satisfied to raise your youngster so that he or she someday can function adequately in a sheltered workshop, you ought to look into adopting these children," the assembled group was told. Some 5 per cent of retarded children are so profoundly affected, they will need nursery care. Yet there exist parents who have discovered the satisfactions to be found in raising these youngsters.

❋ Frank and Verona Paulson raised five biologic children

and cared for more than twenty foster children before they adopted Sandra, a retarded child. At the meeting, Mrs. Paulson rose to describe their experiences with Sandra. "Sandra was placed with us in foster care while adoptive plans were being made for her," she said. "By the time she was three months old, we suspected she was not developing properly. She was too good. Whatever you did with her was all right. She didn't cry to be fed, she didn't cry to be held . . . she lay there. It wasn't natural.

✳"As soon as Sandra was diagnosed retarded, we asked the agency if we could adopt her. We knew she wouldn't leave us, as our other foster infants did, within three or four months. I will not keep a baby in foster care longer than that; we'd get too attached to the child and would be unable to let her go. So, if Sandra was going to be with us—and I doubted anyone would come forward to ask for her—I wanted to be sure she was ours and make some long-range plans for her future."

It wasn't that easy. The agency insisted on doing a total work-up on the little girl, including an evaluation of the child's potential. It took three years before they agreed to allow the Paulsons to adopt the child. They were very trying years. As a rule, retarded children are very generous with their affection. Sandra was typical—a smiling, loving child. She captured the Paulsons' hearts. They feared she'd be taken from them.

Now seven years old, "Sandra is a joy in our life. All the little things she learns to do are high points that cannot be explained to anyone who hasn't had to care for such a child, but they cannot be equaled," her mother says.

✳A father who joined the mothers on the panel underlined this: "When our older child, a normal, healthy boy, took his first steps, we came from all over the house to witness it and to applaud him. When our retarded son took his first steps, we ran out and called in the whole street." The man added, "Neighbors must be educated to accept and to help the retarded child but not to pity him. You cannot raise a human being in dignity with pity."

❋"Expectations" are very important to advocates of normalizing programs for the mentally retarded. Though they are among the first to concede there still is no sure cure for mental retardation, they nevertheless feel that virtually every retarded person has some learning and training potential that can be tapped, an expectation seldom found at large institutions.

❋ Frank Paulson, Sandra's father, cites this as the retarded child's gift to the family: "The satisfaction of knowing that whatever level your child attains, he'd not have got that far had he been institutionalized. You've made an important contribution to the life of another human being. When you look back on your days as God's creatures in this world, that has got to give you contentment."

❋At the meeting's close, organization members offered a list of guidelines, born of experience, for the use of adoption workers who must attempt to judge whether prospective adopters could be successful parents to retarded children. "Look for an affectionate family," suggested the discussion leader. "Look for men and women who have patience, for they will have to do a lot of things repetitively. . . . They should be gregarious and outgoing rather than quiet. Talking to a retarded child is very important. You've got to get them to move. . . . It is better to place a retarded child in a home where there are other youngsters than in a childless setting. Retarded children learn so much from siblings, and your normal child gains in understanding. . . . Finally, seek out families with a strong religious faith, so the retarded child never feels alone."

❋A more detailed list of the basic qualities of successful adopters of mentally retarded children is given by Ursula M. Gallagher, adoption specialist with the U. S. Children's Bureau, in an article that discusses "The Adoption of Mentally Retarded Children." With slight modifications, these characteristics might apply to all who must decide whether to adopt the child with special needs. The list is quoted in its entirety:

1. They [adoptive parents] emphasize *giving* to a child rather than *receiving* from him. They want to reach out to help the child who most needs help. Many are moved by religion and a desire to make a special effort to "love their neighbor."

2. They have a healthy attitude toward mental retardation [substitute name of any handicap] based on sound information. They are not unduly afraid of the problems it may bring.

3. They do not want to adopt a child as an "extension of self." (Frequently, they will already have natural or adopted children with whom they have good relationships.)

4. They expect no more of the child in school or on a job than he can achieve. They will not be embarrassed or frustrated by a child who requires special education or is near the bottom of his class. His social adjustment will mean far more to them than his academic or professional success. They will not expect him to become a physician or a lawyer or a schoolteacher.

5. They feel secure in accepting a child with limitations and can cope with the questions of relatives, neighbors, and friends.

6. They are able and willing to accept a child who is more than normally dependent on them, but they will encourage the child to develop his ability to help himself.

7. They have patience beyond that of most parents. They are satisfied with small, slow gains and rejoice at gradual improvements. They have high tolerance to frustration.

8. They are flexible and can change both their short- and long-term plans for the child.

This last point is dramatically, though atypically, illustrated in the following true story of a Canadian farm couple who, fifteen years ago, adopted a child for whom few of their friends and neighbors held any hopes. A seven-year-old boy, he had spent the years since his birth in an institution for the retarded. His IQ had tested out at thirty-three. Having had and raised a family early, the man and wife found themselves able, and happy, to care for a young person. They could offer a child love, care, space, and, in his father's words, "fresh air, fresh milk, and fresh vegetables." Today, this adopted son is in his second year of medical school. His mother comments, "I hate to think what he might have grown to be if he'd tested out normal."

Single-Parent Adoption

In the world of adoption, the single parent generally is low man (more frequently, woman) on the totem pole, to be considered for adoptive parenthood only when a stable, two-parent family cannot be found to provide a permanent home for a waiting child. Since the numbers of married couples seeking to adopt healthy infant children of all races are much greater than the numbers of infants born and available for adoption today, the unmarried adoptive applicant must be prepared to parent a youngster who's been categorized "hard to place" or "a child with special needs." Generally, this means the single applicant will be offered an older child belonging to a minority racial group. She must be willing to cope with the problems such a child may bring to what more than likely has been a quiet, well-ordered home.

After four years as an adoptive mother of a transracial daughter, now nine years old, Dr. Barbara Feinberg is still coping. "When I adopted Elena, I got the whole bag in one person—older, transracial, a child raised in a religion different from mine, a product of several foster homes only the last of which she remembers with any clarity. She certainly was a challenge," she says.

Yet Dr. Feinberg, a respected educator in her late forties, was not looking for a challenge when she phoned her city's Bureau of Child Welfare to learn about the possibility of becoming an adoptive parent. An only child whose parents no longer are living, she was, in her words, "motivated by a desire to be fundamentally important to another human being—to care for some person and to have that person care about me."

She is quite candid in discussing the factors that led her to adopt: "In general, there are several life options available to women like me—single, career women who have reached middle age—and I was aware of them," she explained in her office, the walls hung with an impressive number of degrees and certificates of academic achievement, the desk cluttered with papers, books, and several pictures of Elena: a striking child with bright blue eyes set against skin the color of a deep suntan. Elena sitting . . . Elena smiling . . . Elena looking soulful and particularly lovely. "I could have gone whole hog for my career, lining up out-of-town lecture dates, writing papers for the trade journals. I could have gotten involved in a long-term affair with the kind of man who doesn't marry; there are enough of them around. I could have started playing surrogate aunt to the children of my friends. I chose instead to devote myself to a child of my own and, with all of its problems, I'm happy I made that decision."

The decision was perhaps the easiest part of the entire process, for it took a year and a half and several social workers before Barbara Feinberg was approved by the agency. Since one-parent adoptions are a relatively new aspect of the adoption business, social workers in those few agencies that have accepted the principle of placement with a single parent remain cautious. Many are not as yet comfortable with the idea, therefore tend to be inflexible in bending the criteria they have set up for such placements. These include existence of an extended family (adults who will be grandparents, uncles, and aunts to the child) and, particularly in the case of boys, of a father figure to serve as a role model for sexual identification. While a number of studies have shown that male children with an emotionally mature mother can be expected to develop an appropriate sexual identity based on her encouragement of appropriate masculine behavior plus the role concepts they derive from outside influences—TV, movies, books, their friends and classmates, others in the community—this requirement proved a temporary stumbling block for Dr. Feinberg. Lacking any immediate family, male or female, she finally produced a distant male relative whose presence eventually satisfied the authorities. In actual practice, Barbara Feinberg has found her friends of both sexes more helpful and more supportive than this relative, and advises professionals in the adoption field to keep an open mind on the extended family qualification, looking into other relationships that may be as helpful.

What of Elena during this time? The progeny of a white mother and black father, both college graduates who were married—but not to one another, she spent her early years in a series of foster homes. Although she was a healthy infant, and attractive, her biracial status made her unadoptable in the small-town community in which she lived. Eventually, she was put into foster care with an elderly black couple. A second foster child completed the household. As she approached her fifth birthday, Elena was looked on as a desperate case, a child who was growing too old to be adoptable. At this point, even a single parent could be considered.

Barbara Feinberg is typical of single persons who seek to adopt a child in that she had no wish for an infant or toddler. Because she must work to support herself, she could not fit her life to an infant's schedule. Ideally, such people apply for a child old enough to spend part of the day in school or, in those neighborhoods where they exist, in a day care situation.

This problem was highlighted in *Children,* in which Los Angeles social worker Ethel Branham noted, "Placing children for adoption with women who are employed full time is another break with traditional adoption practice. But today the working mother is commonplace. The agency [Los Angeles County Department of Adoptions, which began placing children with single parents in 1965] has therefore not regarded such employment as a sufficient reason for keeping a warm, emotionally stable woman from becoming a parent of a child desperately in need of a home of his own. It does, of course, look into the adoptive applicant's plan for providing child care while she is at work."

School was essential to the child care plan she had worked out when she first contemplated motherhood. Dr. Feinberg, therefore, had requested an eight-year-old daughter. Elena was not quite five when it was decided that she must be placed, and at once. So Barbara Feinberg put aside her best laid plans and improvised another set of blueprints. Elena came quickly to her new home and new mother.

It would be nice to add, "They lived happily ever after," at this point in the story, but the initial adjustment was typical of older child adoption. Elena did not fit easily into her new life pattern: a country child, she was constrained by city life and homesick for her foster family. At the same time her new mother was beset with feelings of inadequacy. "First of all, I had a crash course in pediatrics," she recalls. "In short order, Elena came down with chicken pox followed by a whale of a cold. After that, she just kept on crying. And so did I.

"My supervisors were extremely helpful in reworking my teaching schedule so that I was able to take two weeks off to spend with Elena as soon as she arrived. It

was a very rough period. Around dinnertime each night
she'd be overwhelmed with loneliness, especially for the
other child in the foster home, whom she thought of as
her sister. Although I wanted a break with her past, I suggested she write to her. Several times she took pencil and
paper—I offered to help her, of course—but the letter
never got finished.

"She quickly learned how to get at me, testing my
breaking point. One way was to bang her shoes on my
coffee table, marring the finish. As a single professional
woman, I had a very tidy, comfortable apartment. I stood
her misbehavior for quite a while—too long, I now think—
and finally decided I had to draw the line. 'This is
enough. I'll take no more of this,' I shouted. How has having a daughter changed me? For one thing, I've been
amazed to discover I can scream." The teacher smiles in
recollection, and adds, "I also didn't realize I had a lot of
the Jewish mother in me until I found myself reacting to
Elena's not eating."

Elena was born to Protestant parents. Her last foster
family was of the Protestant faith. Barbara Feinberg is
Jewish. "While not observant, being Jewish means something to me," she says. The law in the state in which the
Feinbergs live holds that a child may be placed across
religious lines if the commissioner of child welfare certi-
fies that all attempts have been made to place the youngster within her own religion. Obviously, this may be taken
quite literally, which often results in children remaining in custodial care until they reach adulthood, or with
flexibility. Dr. Feinberg discovered that Elena knew the
days of the week because of Sunday. Periodically, the little girl asked to go to church. Her requests were granted.
Now, four years later, "When she's angry with me, she's
Christian; when she likes me, she's Jewish," her mother
reports.

The greater community has reacted very well to single-parent adoptions. Many mothers tell of lavish "baby showers" given by friends and relatives after their adopted children came home to live. One young woman recalled, "I didn't have to buy my child a new dress for more than a year; she received so many presents from so many people. I hardly knew many of them, but they were so excited for me; they just wanted to do something."

Barbara's experience underlines this community concern. "My co-workers gave a large party for us; Elena has more children's books than she'll ever have time to read . . . and dolls . . . and games. Friends presented us with new things and hand-me-downs, in good condition, from their children. So much attention was focused on us, it was an effort to come down to reality, especially for the child who wasn't accustomed to material possessions."

During their first two weeks together, Dr. Feinberg had to make plans for Elena's care so that she could return to work. A day care center answered the need. "I enrolled her because it seemed the most convenient arrangement," says her mother, "but it proved a wise choice. To this day, even though she's been taught differently, part of Elena believes that her foster mother is the lady out of whose tummy she came. She has trouble defining the differences in the terms biologic, foster, and adoptive. The day care situation was a good one in that, while there were a number of caring adults involved, it did not introduce yet another mother figure in her already confused life."

Elena now attends a public school where she is doing well. ("She may be an underachiever," according to her mother, whose academic standards are high for Elena, as they are for herself.) And she is more involved in social life than in social studies. This interest has brought about a dramatic change in Dr. Feinberg's life. Whereas she is naturally a private person who is content to stay at home reading a book or listening to records, Elena's mother finds herself having to be more socially active than in the past. At first, she planned a full slate of activities for each weekend that she and Elena would spend together. The two of them would either be going to visit someone or some place or company would have been invited to their home. They still were not comfortable with one another; outsiders relieved the tension. Now they have learned to live quietly together, but Elena's exuberance has rubbed off on her mother. "I do more hostessy things now than I used to before Elena was a part of my life," says Barbara Feinberg. "I see more people and I find that I like many more people I meet." A friend confided, "Barbara is a much softer person since she became a mother."

Children are great solvers of their own problems. Elena is no exception. To cope with the needs of a little girl being raised in a fatherless household, she has invented a Rent-a-Daddy Plan under which she inveigles any number of her mother's male friends and business associates to go kite flying or bike riding with her. Every once in a while she will ask one, "Why don't you marry my Mommy and become my Daddy?" Her mother considers those moments "a bit embarrassing—but I've learned to handle that problem, too."

David and Daniel, teen-age brothers adopted by a single male parent, don't need a Rent-a-Mommy Plan in their lives. Their new father, thirty-six-year-old Peter Di-Andreas, married Jeanette, twenty-seven, one year after the boys came to live with him in the spacious suburban home he shared with his parents, an elderly couple of Greek ancestry. The wedding photos show a handsome couple: he, a darkish blond man of medium build, somewhat stocky; she, about the same height with long brown hair and an easy smile. The ushers, good-looking boys with auburn hair, fashionably long, and freckles scattered across up-tilted noses, are a bit young to be wedding attendants, but protocol is winked at when you're attending the wedding of your own, brand-new parents. All in all, they are pictures of a fairy tale finish to a story of adoption that could have made use of a fairy godmother or two somewhere along the way.

When the tale began, Pete (an outgoing, easy-to-know fellow, who is quick to have acquaintances relate to him on a first-name basis) was not a young man in search of a child to make his life complete. In fact, he had no idea that he'd become a statistic among the small number of single men who are becoming adoptive parents. (Agencies that place children with single parents cite a ratio of some twenty-five placements with females to one placement with a male.) What he had in common with those other men is that he liked children. "I've always liked kids and have worked with them, in one way or another, during much of my life," he explained. As a teen-ager, Pete supervised youth groups at the YMCA. In the Army, he volunteered his services to an orphanage in Korea. When he returned to civilian life, it seemed natural for him to stop in at a Catholic home for boys in his town and ask if they could put some of his spare time to good use. He worked five days a week as office manager of a medium-sized paper-goods firm, he explained, but could volunteer a weekday evening or two, or take some of the boys on outings during weekends.

Pete became a familiar figure at the institution, which houses boys aged eight to fourteen whose own families cannot care for them. Weekends, some of the residents went home for visits. Others maintained tenuous ties with their parents. And there were some, like David and Daniel, who never went to any home other than the one responsible for their custodial care. Upon inquiry, Pete learned the boys had not had any contact with their parents for many years. For young men, they had been in an astounding number of custodial institutions and foster homes. Permanent scars on their bodies are ever-present reminders of child abuse suffered during the earliest months of their lives. To add to these appalling facts, the older of the two boys, David, was fast approaching fourteen, the age at which he would have to leave the home for yet another residence. For the first time in their lives, the brothers would be separated.

To Pete, who always had enjoyed a happy home life, the idea of this separation was disturbing. He began to take the boys home with him for weekend visits. "I liked the fact that they were teen-agers," Pete recalls. "We had an instant relationship. They liked to play ball, go boating and fishing—all things I like to do. I could never have become involved with younger children—I'm not a baby-sitter—but the boys fit right in with my own life-style. One day, without giving much thought to the idea before I blurted it out, I asked them, 'How would you like to make this relationship permanent?' As soon as I said it, I knew it was right. That way, they would never have to be taken from one another. I liked them, and my parents liked them. It just seemed right."

The brothers thought the idea was fine but, because they had never been released for adoption, they just assumed it couldn't be done. They were almost right.

That Sunday evening, when Pete dropped the boys off at the home, he spoke of his plan to several members of the staff. Nobody applauded. He was single . . . a man . . . and the boys were not free for adoption. He mentioned it again at his next visit. To his surprise, the same officials who had always been most welcoming of his time and attention now greeted with hostility his decision to adopt the boys. As if he'd contracted a dread disease, Pete quickly became *persona non grata* at the home. "Instead of saying, 'How great!' everyone had a negative response handy: 'Why do you want to do this?'" Pete says, "I was single—and a man. People began to wonder what was wrong with me. Funny, they didn't have the same doubts when they encouraged me to take the boys for weekend outings."

Peter DiAndreas is a mild man; he wouldn't hurt a gopher, and there are many of them on his property, digging up the garden he so carefully planted in the tree-shaded area just beyond a small stone fountain centered on the front lawn. But he is a determined man. He could offer the boys a much better life than the one they had. He had room for them in his house. He had the means to put them through school. He thought he had the understanding they needed. In his words, "I was not going to allow these people, intent on keeping the stipend they were allotted for each child in their care, to stop me from doing something I was convinced was right. There had to be a way to break down the wall they'd erected. I was set on finding that way."

After a number of false starts—phone calls and letters that did nothing to further his cause—Pete contacted his local branch of COAC (Council on Adoptable Children). When they had heard his story, they referred him to a competent attorney who was experienced in working his way through the legalisms involved in freeing children from foster care to make them available for adoption.

While Pete credits his lawyer for the success of his suit to get the brothers, there were many difficulties in store. "The red tape we had to go through would take four hours to describe," says Pete. "And some of the questions that the social worker put to me—and to Jeanette, because by then we had met and become engaged—were unbelievable. They questioned our fertility—could we have children?—which seemed beside the point, since we weren't looking to adopt an infant or any child who was otherwise in demand. They checked the dimensions of the rooms the boys would occupy, even their beds, when in the institution the brothers lived crowded in with others in a dormitory. They even checked the kind of milk we keep in the house." Pete stresses that, attorney and all, he never would have been able to adopt any child from the institution—although there are many who should be given the opportunity for homes and families of their own—had he asked for just any child. What was in his favor was that he was asking for two specific children whose history he knew. Because they had not been in contact with their parents since a stormy infancy, nor had any interest been expressed in reuniting the family, Pete knew they had a legal right, in his state, to be surrendered for adoption. On his suggestion I phoned the home, claiming to be interested in adopting a boy in their care. None were available, they answered.

Few people would have the fortitude to fight the system as Pete did. Others might not be able to afford the battle. Pete estimates the entire cost of the adoption, legal and court fees, at some $3,700—a lot of money for a workingman.

When the courtship of the boys was over and the reality of day-to-day living set in, it didn't set in smoothly, not for Pete, nor for David and Daniel. Raised in communal living, the brothers found it difficult to deal with the concept of things that belonged to them jointly and individually. "In the home, whatever you wore was put into the laundry hamper," David recalls. "After the clothes were cleaned, they were stored in a common closet. Whenever any of us needed something, he'd just go over and pick out clothing for the day."

Pete tells how the boys would eye the refrigerator, tentatively inquire, "May I go get something to eat?" They had to be reassured that, barring its being close to dinnertime, they could snack at will. Their favorite activity still may be going to the supermarket for the week's groceries. At first, as they had reacted to raiding the refrigerator, they would ask, "May we buy this?" or "Is it okay if we have some of that?" "Now"—Jeanette pops her head out of the kitchen to add—"they don't ask, and you should see some of the stuff they pile into the shopping cart. . . . They also like to help in the kitchen, something they'd never been permitted to do before." While we speak, Daniel is cutting melon balls for a fruit salad.

"I was very careful with what I bought for them when they first came to live with me," Pete went on. "Even though I knew most kids their age had their own bikes, transistor radios, and other possessions, I held off. I wasn't going to buy their affection, but I knew they needed mine—so there was more giving of affection than of gifts." And the affection was returned. "Even today," Jeanette said, "David, who's fifteen, won't go out with the garbage without giving me a good-by kiss."

The problems of sibling rivalry, common to every household, were magnified in the DiAndreas home as both brothers vied for their new father's attention. In the custodial homes, there had been little to compete for. Now Pete was the big prize, and the brothers fought constantly. "That was our biggest problem," Pete recalls. "It still hasn't settled down to the point where I'm comfortable with it. While each wanted to lay claim to me, they were leery of forming relationships that last. This hesitancy extended to the young fellows in the neighborhood. David and Daniel had to learn to relax their guard and accept friendship. At the home, it seems, they didn't do this because so many of the boys they came to like were reassigned elsewhere, or David and Daniel would be sent to a new residence and have to get used to different surroundings and a completely new group of people, young and old."

As a single parent, before he was married, Pete worried about what mischief his sons would be into during school holidays and summer vacations. To fill the holiday hours, he made up work lists, figuring that a busy child

was a safe child. "All the windows in the house have to
be washed today," he'd say. On rainy days, he'd call
from the office frequently to find out what the boys were
up to. (Pete's mother had passed away after a brief illness
and his father was away at work.) His summer plan was
to send Daniel, the younger son, to a nearby day camp
with a good teen-age program. Daniel balked at first, but
after a week he loved camp. To keep David occupied,
Pete lined up projects for him in the neighborhood: mow-
ing lawns, doing paint jobs. Even with all this planning,
Pete would rush home from work to find Daniel, who'd
come back from camp only to have an argument with
David, walking down the road and crying.

Daniel proved to be his biggest problem and his biggest
test. He came to the DiAndreas home equipped with a
vocabulary that would be a source of pride to a long-
shoreman—but was a source of dismay here, where pro-
fanity was unacceptable. "I'm a strict disciplinarian," says
Pete, "although I don't go in for corporal punishment.
My sons have enough scars over their bodies to last
them a lifetime. But, frankly, I didn't know what to do
with Daniel. His handwriting and spelling were poor, so
I came up with the the idea of making his punishment a
writing assignment, something like 'I will not use swear
words again' one hundred times, with a twofold purpose.
It improved his writing—both boys have made great scho-
lastic strides since they came from the institution, where
they were labeled underachievers—but not his behavior.
Jeanette and I had a saying that David was the apple of
my eye, while Daniel was the gray hair on my chest. But
I was getting grayer than I liked.

"In addition to his foul language, Daniel had a run-
ning battle with my father, whose authority he would not
accept. I thought, 'I asked for some of this, but my father
doesn't have to put up with it' and . . . despite all I went
through to get custody of the boys, there came a day, be-

fore their adoption was finalized, when I'd had it with Daniel and I resolved to take him back to where I got him. I even drove up to the home, without Daniel, as a trial run. When I looked at the building, I realized I couldn't do it. I had made a permanent commitment to another human being. Together, we would have to work our problems out. I think we're doing that."

While it is usual for the single male parent to adopt a male child, as Peter DiAndreas took David and Daniel for his sons, and for the female who has no marital partner to ask for a little girl, forming a family such as Barbara Feinberg and Elena make up, there are single-parent adoptions that cross lines of sex. A caseworker with an Eastern social service agency tells with pleasure of having placed a five-year-old girl with a bachelor who makes his home in the Southern section of the country. In this case, the worker was satisfied that the child had sufficient contact with female figures. The bachelor's mother, a woman in her early sixties, adores children and comes by to visit her new granddaughter several times a week. Additionally, a female housekeeper is employed, weekdays, to take care of the cleaning and cooking and to be at home when the little girl arrives from school.

Though it receives more publicity than is warranted by fact, the problem of homosexuality is considered by those who must deal with single-parent adoption. Doubts center around male applicants more than they do female, perhaps because of the mystique that women naturally harbor maternal feelings. But the unmarried man who wants to parent a child is looked upon as, somehow, unnatural. Professionals who have placed children with single parents believe this concern is overemphasized, and say they can discern an applicant's motives during the series of interviews that are an integral part of the adoption process.

New York papers recently reported the story of Ben,

v-one-year-old homosexual who has been trying to
ﾟ a youngster for some time. Ben and Joseph have
been living together for eleven years. That's a longer time,
Ben pointed out, than the marriages of Joseph's brother
and sister, both of whom are divorced. "I like children,"
Ben said, as he explained why he wants to have a child.
"I've seen so many neglected children. I feel like a kid has
to be taken care of. I'd like to give a kid a chance." Any
boy he could adopt, says Ben, would have his own room
in the brownstone shared by Ben and Joseph. He'd go to
school and probably have enough money for luxuries as
well as necessities. And, Ben adds, his parents would
love him.

Thus far, Ben has been discouraged by the agencies to
which he has applied. Commenting on the case, a psy-
choanalyst who is the consultant for a large private adoption agency said, "There are homosexual marriages that
are well adjusted. In those cases one could envision that
raising a child might be all right. But the child would
have to face a difficulty in terms of sexual identity. And I
don't know if it could be overcome." At this point,
placement of a child with an acknowledged homosexual
parent seems unlikely.

And, while the idea of single-parent adoption itself is
gaining acceptance, there are fears that, in practice, the
number of such placements made annually will decrease.
Marlena Davis, an extremely articulate black woman who
is the adoptive single mother of Cassandra, now five, has
applied for a second little girl at the same agency from
which her daughter came to her some three years ago.
Miss Davis has proven her competence as a mother and
ought to be able to expect a second daughter soon, since
what she is asking for is a black child beyond the infant
stage of her life.

"Cassie keeps asking for a sister," she told me. "She
used to ask me to get her a daddy, but it turned out she

was more interested in one as a means of obtaining a sibling than as a man in her own life or in mine. So I've put in my application for another child, but I have doubts about whether Cassie will be able to get the sister she wants. In the few years since Cassie came to live with me, more married couples have come forward to accept black children—and older children—in their lives. And the agencies have not changed so much in their thinking that they will place a child with a single person when there's a couple waiting." Children with special needs are available, but for most single parents, who must go out to their jobs, adopting such children is out of the question. The youngsters require more time and attention than these adults are able to give.

It is still too early to learn how children who have been adopted into one-parent homes have fared in growing up. Recent studies have shown that the child whose adoptive parents live comfortably with the fact of adoption, accepting its differences from biological parenthood, grows to be a more secure adult. It is unlikely that the single adoptive parent will pretend biologic parenthood to her child, a pretense made even the more difficult if the child is several years old at the time of adoption and so remembers both his past and his entrance into what then becomes his permanent home. It follows that these children ought to have the strength that comes with feeling secure in one's home.

In the outside world, Dr. Feinberg finds that her daughter tends to make close friends with children in a similar situation, those who are being raised by a single parent because of a death in the family, a separation, or a divorce. "But that isn't unnatural," she explains, "because these are many of the children who will be found enrolled in day care and after-school centers. Elena is not alone."

Certainly in a nation where one out of every three marriages ends in divorce, millions of youngsters are being raised in what, for all intents and purposes, are one-parent families, a Saturday visit with Father or Mother notwithstanding. The child adopted into a single-parent home will not have to suffer the tensions of children of divorce. In this day, that may not be a small point to consider.

Adopting Your Foster Child

Following his father's sudden death in an automobile accident, John's mother found herself unable to cope with the financial burden of raising three young children as well as with the emotional shock of widowhood. She suffered a breakdown. John and his two sisters were placed with a foster family as a temporary means of care until that day when their mother would be well enough to resume her responsibilities and be reunited with her children.

Eleven-month-old Tonine was found crying in the crib she'd been tied to by her mother, a heroin addict, who had then gone out, leaving the little girl alone in their two-room apartment. The woman had not reappeared for two days when aroused neighbors called the police, who took the infant from this home in which she'd been so neglected. Tonine's father is unknown. Now four years old, Tonine has been living with a foster family for the past three years. Her mother, who has visited her twice in these three years—each time without notice—remains dependent on drugs. She cannot care for her daughter nor will she release the child for adoption.

Tonine's foster parents live in fear that this little girl, who is growing so well in their loving home, will someday be taken from them.

Freddy's mother never took her child from the hospital in which he was born prematurely, weighing less than five pounds. He was still in the incubator when she walked out, abandoning the infant. Efforts to locate her proved fruitless. Neighbors guessed she might have gone back home, somewhere in the South, they didn't know just where. Freddy, who has been in three foster homes in his six long years of life, now resides in an institution for disturbed boys. To the viewer who peers at him through a one-way mirror, Freddy seems a calm child, sitting in solitude and turning the pages of a picture book. The visitor has been asked to keep his distance, however, for Freddy jumps, startled, and cowers when approached by any man he has not learned to trust. It is suspected that Freddy suffered abuse by a man in his second foster home and was therefore unable to adjust to the third. Women fare better with Freddy.

Stella was born with cerebral palsy. Unable to accept the idea of raising the child, Stella's young parents asked that the little girl be placed in foster care, some place where they could visit her, study her development, and make up their minds as to whether they would ever be able to cope with the child and her illness in their own home.

Caseworkers have high hopes that John's mother one day will be able to resume care of her children. They are working with Stella's parents, who are both guilty and apprehensive; they don't know if the couple will be able to provide the strong support and the love this little girl will need. Tonine and Freddy are among the children in limbo, more than 300,000 it is estimated, for whom foster care has become a way of life.

Social agencies generally are agreed on the proper uses of foster care. They see it as temporary care, an interim solution while permanent plans are made for the child's welfare. The ideal is to rehabilitate the biologic family, whether their problem is physical or mental illness, drugs or poverty, and return the child to his home. Only when such attempts fail, they believe, should arrangements be made for permanent placement of the child, preferably in an adoptive home.

The unhappy reality runs counter to declared social work policy. Foster care is "temporary" for less than a third of the children who come under this system. In a study on foster children, Dr. David Fanshel of Columbia's School of Social Work found: "The major exodus of children under [foster] care occurs during the first year of entry, when three out of ten children leave. Thereafter, there is a rapid decline in the number of children discharged, so that after three and a half years it has become only a modest outflow and most of the children then in care seem destined to spend their remaining years of childhood as foster children."

The children's experiences vary as do the homes into which they are placed. George B., now a transit policeman with two children of his own, one bio-child and one adopted, experienced both the bad and the good in his eighteen years as a foster child. "In one of the early homes I was put in," he recalls, "the lady treated me and my brothers like dirt. You should see the slop she fed us; she even put us at a table away from her own family, who ate the steak while we got the grits. She was only in it for the money," he says angrily, as if this were yesterday's event. "Then, on the day of the social worker's visit, she'd dress us up in clothes we'd never had on before, in cheap new shoes that had never covered our feet, to show what a good job she was doing in taking care of us poor little boys. Luckily, we were only there for three or four years, and then the agency moved us out. Although I was separated from my brothers, the next family I was placed with was very kind. I was lucky. I stayed with them until I went into the army, and I still keep in touch. They're like relatives to me; they're good people."

"Like relatives"—but not like parents. The concept of impermanence upon which foster care is based makes the building of a secure relationship between child and foster parent almost impossible. Even the best foster parents must maintain some distance for fear of becoming so emotionally entangled that they will not be able to give up the child should the time come for separation. For the child, "the sense of being on loan makes it hard to make an emotional commitment." Thus was foster care described by columnist Art Buchwald, who spoke from his own experience to an audience assembled to celebrate the one hundred and fiftieth anniversary of the Jewish Child Care Association. Only six when his mother died, Buchwald was placed in an orphan asylum. "After six weeks," he recalled, "it was decided I would make a swell foster child." He and his three sisters were first sent to the same family. Then Buchwald was separated from his sisters and placed in a succession of foster homes. He went on, "So at the age of seven I said, 'The hell with it—I think I'll be a humorist.' I could turn everything into a joke, including my social worker.

"If you're a grownup who pokes fun at authority, society pays you vast sums of money. As a child, if you poke fun at authority, they beat your brains out."

Today, persons in authority *are* taking a closer look at the foster care situation. Before citations are awarded, however, let us look at some of the factors that have led to this growing awareness of the situation of the hundreds of thousands of children who have been described as "orphans of the living."

The current scarcity of adoptable healthy infants has had a twofold effect on unearthing available youngsters among the children who wait. Would-be parents seeking to adopt children learned of the existence of many youngsters who could be made available for adoption. Many couples approached the foster care departments of social agencies, inquiring about these children. At the same time, many social workers found themselves having to devote less time to case loads of newborn babies (simply, there weren't many) and thus were able to spend more time dealing with the complex issues of freeing foster children for adoption and placing them in permanent homes. Time and staff continue to affect the progress of placement. In 1972, California's Open Door Society of Riverside and San Bernardino counties reported, "The California Association of Adoption Agencies estimates that well over 6,000 of the 32,000 children now in foster care could readily be legally freed and made available to adoptive parents.

"Last year, Los Angeles County adoptions freed for adoption 396 children referred to them by the Department of Probation—more than ever before. Right now Riverside County adoptions are working on freeing 117 children. San Bernardino County states they could keep three social workers and one attorney busy full time, but they are allowed only enough money to hire one worker, whose job involves checking out all the possible family ties of a youngster in a foster home. At this rate thousands of children who could have homes won't because of the monetary cutbacks and restrictions placed on the agencies. . . ."

Penny-wise, pound foolish. In 1972 a federal commission reported $35,000 as the amount it costs a typical American family to raise a child to the age of eighteen.

hat same year, professors David Fanshel and Eugene B.
uinn of the Columbia School of Social Work gave the
cost of raising one foster child in New York City from infancy to age eighteen as $122,500, almost four times the
"family member" figure.

The previously quoted statement by the Open Door
Society, which places the blame for not freeing more children for adoption on monetary cutbacks, also cites as
blameworthy ". . . a lack of knowledge and concern on
the part of us—the adults who have the power to influence
the situation."

The recognition of that power is one of the more recent
developments in the world of adoption and foster care.
For years foster parents served in silence. Many social
agencies that depended upon them to come through in
a time of crisis in a child's life nevertheless looked upon
the foster parents as people able to care for a child but
not good enough to adopt. Those families who had foster
children in their care feared to speak up lest the children
they'd grown to love would be removed from their homes.
These concerns were not unfounded. One agency had a
reputed "policy" of removing youngsters from their foster homes every two years so that foster parent and foster child would not become too "attached" to one another.
Anthologies could have been filled with tales of other
forced separations. David Pilliod, an energetic and en-
lightened caseworker with the New York Foundling Hospital, refers to this as the real crisis in foster care. He explains, "For a long time, and even now, workers saw
foster care defined as 'temporary care,' whereas many foster parents came to view the situation, after a while, as
parents. Should they become Mom and Dad, Aunt and
Uncle, or Grandma and Grandpa? If they commit themselves wholly, isn't it likely they will be hurt?"

"We attempt to recruit as foster parents people who
have an adoptive potential," says Charles Solomon, di-

rector of the Foster Home Division of New York's Jewish Child Care Association. "But we can't make them any promises because we can't be absolutely certain we won't run up against obstacles in getting the child freed. But those foster parents who see this kind of care as a means toward adoption don't really hear what we say. For the children," he adds, "this situation is worse than terrible—if there's any such word."

Some recent court decisions in the handling of children involved in tugs of war between biologic parents and long-term foster parents seem to call for a word that means "something worse than terrible." Across the country, legal decisions have varied as widely as the whims of the judges.

In Mineola, Long Island, New York State Supreme Court Justice Alexander Berman ruled in favor of removing a nine-year-old child from the one foster home she'd been in since infancy and awarded her to her biologic parents, who showed they were now free of the addiction to heroin that had made them incapable of caring for their child. The judge could not deny that "there may be severe emotional conflicts" that will beset a child "who is confronted with the tragic and traumatic experience of being removed from a home where she has been for such a long period of time." But, he added, the courts have held "the status of natural parents is so important that in determining the best interests of the child, it may counterbalance, even outweigh, superior material and cultural advantages which may be afforded by adoptive parents."

That same year, Family Court Judge Michael DeCiantis of Providence, Rhode Island, ruled against the request of a six-year-old girl's natural mother to be given custody of the child, deciding that to take the youngster from parents with whom she lived for more than five and a half years "would be a shock worse than kidnaping. Nothing could be more cruel." The judge criticized both the natural mother and the state child welfare services for a lack of interest in, and attention for, the child.

Such disparate rulings have caused traditionally reticent groups of foster parents to speak out. "If the court is going to be a natural mothers' court, it should be named that way," said one foster mother currently battling to retain custody of a child whose drug-addicted mother is attempting to reclaim him after having signed a surrender form. "But it's called children's court," she went on, "and the rights of the children should be uppermost."

"Foster parents have been made to feel they are on a plane lower than adoptive parents and adoptive parents have been considered second class citizens by many persons," said Flora Cunha of O.F.F.E.R. (Organization of Foster Families for Equality and Reform). Mrs. Cunha successfully adopted her foster daughter fourteen years ago. She and her husband are adoptive parents to four young people. "As a group, we are not foster parents for the money and we would like to shift the emphasis from the money aspect to the child," she said.

Across the country, dedicated foster parents such as these are now joining with other groups concerned with the rights of children. Pressured by these lobbies, legislators in many states have forced through changes aimed at removing children from the limbo of foster care. There are several ways in which this can be accomplished. One traditional means, frequently unenforced due to the extremes of overwork or lethargy, is for the agency to obtain a release from the bio-parent. Another is by asking the court to decide the child has been permanently neglected. This means the parent hasn't shown any interest in the child for a year (sometimes six months is enough for termination of parental rights) even though the parent was physically and financially able to show interest and efforts were made by the agency to strengthen the parent-child relationship. Another way of freeing the child for adoption is by asking the court to decide the youngster is abandoned.

In many states, laws establishing subsidized adoption made possible the adoptions of many children whose foster families were willing, but financially unable, to adopt the children in their care. Not only was subsidized adoption humane legislation, it was economically sound. A study of New York City's child welfare system* found that "while adoption subsidies equal about $1,500 per year for each family, foster care payments are superior: they are higher, they are tax deductible, and supplemented by clothing, medical allowances, and other benefits."

Other legislation, such as New York's twenty-four-month review law, has put pressure on the professionals to review the cases of all children in their custody every two years with an eye either to returning the child to his initial home or setting into motion procedures that will lead to an adoptive home. In theory, a permanent place must be found for each child, so that almost no child would remain in permanent foster care or be moved from home to home to institution as was Freddy, the troubled youngster described at the outset of this chapter. Technically, Freddy could have been declared legally abandoned under statutes that existed on the books. Efforts to place him in an adoptive home could have followed. It was because nobody *looked* at his case file and implemented the laws which were relevant that a review law had to be mandated.

Because of the changing system, many caseworkers now inform a child's parents, at the outset, "You now have one year to plan for your child; after that, we will start proceedings for his release." Several states have Foster Parents Preference bills, under which a family that

* Kathryn Allott and Marlys Harris, "In the Child's Best Interest," 1971, available from the Fund for the City of New York.

has cared for a child for twenty-four months or more
must receive "preference and first consideration" if the
child is freed for adoption.

Not all foster families will take advantage of this preference when it is accorded them. Experience has shown
there are many good people who will commit themselves
to care for a child until he attains adulthood, but who
are unwilling to make the commitment to adopt. In fact,
this is a fairly common situation, in which a child has
been in the same foster home for three to five years and
is suddenly made available for adoption, according to
caseworker David Pilliod. Typically, he finds, "the foster mother wants to adopt the youngster and the foster
father doesn't." This leads Mr. Pilliod to wonder, "What
did the family expect from the relationship and what did
the child deliver?" He is aware that many foster fathers
have some hesitancy about giving a child their name or
of having the adopted boy or girl share with the bio-children in any eventual distribution of a potential estate. If
the foster parents will not adopt, they must at some point
tell the child a permanent home is being sought for him,
one with a good family that will be able to care for him
as their own. The foster care situation at that point becomes a problem of older child adoption.

Those who wonder whether the stress on adoption over
foster care is in many cases a matter of semantics have
only to look at the bold, proud signature of Lester Dorrence, eight-year-old adopted son of Ernest and Bethany
Dorrence, and until last year their foster child. Lester
doodles his adoptive name over and over, in big block letters, in capitals and lower case, even in script, which he is
only beginning to learn to write. When just a given name
will do, Lester Dorrence will use his surname as well.

"I never realized it bothered Lester, having a last
name that was different from ours and from his big brother's," said Ernest Dorrence, a kindly, middle-aged man

who took time during his day off from his job as a sales-
man of grocery items to speak of his younger son. The
Dorrences also have a seventeen year old, Theo. "Lester
always knew he was a foster child, but he also always
knew we loved him. I thought that was enough. But the
day after we went to court to finalize the adoption and
we told Lester he was ours, that we'd adopted him and
he no longer was Lester Pierce but Lester Dorrence now,
he ran to school a half hour before the building opened,
he was that anxious to tell the kids he was a 'real' member
of our family. Evidently, the boys and girls in his class
had questioned him about why he had a different last
name from the rest of the family and it had been bothering him, but he never said anything about it. His teacher
called that day to tell my wife how he'd made the an-
nouncement, standing up before the entire class. When
I heard about it that night, I'll tell you the truth—I cried.
And I was angry at myself, too—because I might never
have made the move to adopt Lester if the social worker
hadn't come by and told us she had a couple interested
in adopting the boy."

"I told her nobody was going to take my baby away,"
said Bethany, smoothing the throw pillows on her lemon-
colored sofa, which was protected by plastic covers from
stains and wear and tear. The furnishings in the small,
comfortable apartment, new and chosen with care, are
being cared for to last. "And then the social worker said
we'd have to do something permanent, that we'd get
preference in any adoption action and the agency would
work with us, but she couldn't justify leaving Lester any
longer in foster care.

"'Okay,' we said, 'tell us what we've got to do.'"

One of the reasons the Dorrences had sought out a
foster child originally, after they learned they could have
no more biologic children, was that they couldn't afford
to adopt a child. They took the risk of having the child

removed from their home in return for the security provided by monthly payments for Lester's keep plus clothing allowances and free medical care. While Ernest's
earnings had improved in the six years since Lester entered their home, the cost of living had risen as well. The
caseworker, aware of their circumstances, informed them
they'd be eligible for adoption subsidy payments, an
amount that varies according to the adopting family's income. She also put them in touch with a lawyer who does
most of the legal work for the agency with which she was
connected.

The lawyer handled the adoption, charging the Dorrences $200, which they paid out as they could. As finan-
cial matters now stand, "We get a monthly check for less
than we did when Lester was a foster child, and we're
responsible for all his expenses including doctor bills
and clothing," explained the boy's father. "I'll be honest
with you. The money helps. We wouldn't have let any-
body take Lester from us even if there wasn't any subsidy. Somehow, with the good Lord's help, we'd have
made it. But I must say this: the extra money gives us a
real boost, and the child doesn't feel the tension of our
worrying when he needs a new pair of shoes."

No caseworker had to prod Joseph and Donna Proust
to adopt Bonnie. The Prousts exemplify many of today's
young couples who run into a dead end traveling the
regular adoption channels and veer toward foster care as
a shorter route to having a child placed in their home.
While agencies are able to separate youngsters likely to
be made available for adoption from those for whom reunion with their own families is foreseen and thus to
place the more likely candidates for adoption with families anxious to adopt, there is no guarantee all will work
out as planned.

A young couple, both in their twenties, the Prousts de-

cided to adopt a child after they learned, in the fourth
year of their marriage, it was unlikely they'd conceive
one. They thought their credentials impressive. Joseph,
a cameraman, was earning a good salary with job security assured him through a powerful trade union. Donna,
a dental hygienist, was honest in stating her intention to
give up her job to raise any children she and Joseph might
adopt. Telephone calls they placed to six different agencies came up with the same response: there was a wait of
from two to five years for a healthy infant. Donna
wouldn't consider any child past two years of age—the
baby's sex was not a factor—because, she says, "We're a
young couple, and I thought I wouldn't feel comfortable
dealing with schools and the problems of the older child.
I had to grow into the role of a mother slowly. I don't feel
that way now, but those were my thoughts when we
started out."

"I believe I could have handled any age child," Joseph
interjects, "as long as it was healthy. We were asked if
we would consider a handicapped child and I was the
one who said no to that. I'm afraid I'd love the child
through pity and I don't want to do that."

So there they were, up against a minimum wait of two
years. Donna wouldn't wait. To know Donna is to understand this at once. The Prousts began to explore alternate
means of adoption. In the course of time, this included
negotiations with a lawyer who promised to deliver a
child, then lost his contact with the unwed mother. A
second lawyer had to retrieve the thousand dollars the
Prousts had been required to place in escrow.

Afraid to attempt independent adoption again, the
Prousts tried a twofold approach: they wrote to an agency
that specialized in intercountry adoption, requesting a
Korean child, and they telephoned a local branch of a
citizens organization composed of adoptive parents who
lobbied for legislation in the field of children's rights and

volunteered to counsel couples interested in adoption. A member of the parents group contacted the Prousts and set a date for a meeting.

After she spoke with Joseph and Donna, the director of the citizens group placed calls to several agencies with whom she had worked co-operatively in the past, asking if there were any healthy children—of any race, for the Prousts had passed that hurdle earlier, even informing their extended families of the possibility of their adopting a black or Oriental child—but a child no older than two years.

"No," came the response from the first two agencies reached. "No, but . . ." said the director of adoptions at the third agency. But . . . there was a little girl in foster care . . . just two years old . . . her mother was Chinese; her father, while unknown, was evidently Caucasian. The child, Bonnie, had been in the same foster home for two years, where she had never been visited by her mother. At a meeting in court, when Bonnie was a year old, the mother said she was not well enough to care for her child, but she would not surrender the baby for adoption. Although she didn't keep an appointment with a psychiatrist, set up on recommendation of the family court judge who had hopes of rehabilitating the young mother, she was allowed another year during which she was to make up her mind: to raise her own daughter or release her. The twelve months had passed—without a word from Bonnie's mother. Her foster mother had become ill. Were the Prousts interested in becoming foster parents to Bonnie, knowing the agency would make every attempt to secure the child's release—knowing, too, they might not be successful?

" 'A 70 per cent chance in favor of adoption' was how the caseworker put it," Joseph recounted. "We said we would like to meet Bonnie."

A meeting was arranged to coincide with Bonnie's ap-

pointment for a medical checkup at the agency. Because
her foster mother still wasn't well, her foster father
brought the little girl in, then waited in an anteroom
while the Prousts were shown to a small playroom.
Bonnie was intent on a block construction. Joseph tried to
involve himself in her activity. "I can't say it was love at
first sight," says Donna. "In fact, she hardly looked at us
at all. Since she didn't yet speak, we couldn't hold a conversation, but she was too big to pick up and hold in my
arms. I felt"—Donna grasps for the word as the experience is re-created, re-experienced—"inept."

Joseph and Donna went home from that meeting with
nothing more definite decided than that there would be a
second meeting. This time, the Prousts took Bonnie to
lunch. "If our first encounter wasn't joy-provoking, our
second was an unmitigated disaster," says Joseph. "Have
you ever taken a two year old to a restaurant? Bonnie
turned over the salt shaker, played with the individual
envelopes of sugar, took the ice cubes from her glass of
water and threw them under the table, alternately laugh-
ing with delight or shrieking when thwarted from whatever mischief she hoped to accomplish. Just getting
through the meal and out of the restaurant was a tri-
umph. It encouraged us to make a third try at a relationship."

The third meeting was more intelligently planned.
Donna and Joseph took Bonnie to the beach for the day.
As the little girl played in the sand, the two grownups
were able to relax and enjoy the contented youngster.
"This is silly," Donna decided, "our assessing this child
like a piece of merchandise." She goes on to explain, "It
suddenly hit me, what we'd been doing: playing peek-a-
boo with a two-year-old child, now you see us, now you
don't. Were we ready to accept the responsibilities of parenthood or not? If not, then we had to stop fooling ourselves and others who'd become involved in our game-

playing. If yes, here was a child. We went home, telephoned Bonnie's foster family, and said we'd like to keep her with us. They said that was fine with them. The next day, we called the agency, told them Bonnie had stayed overnight in our home, that she seemed happy, and we didn't see any sense in continuing to move her around. That's how we became foster parents."

As foster parents, the Prousts received monthly payments toward Bonnie's room, board, and clothing expenses—money they didn't need and which they placed in a bank account in trust for the little girl. They also received monthly visits from a social worker—helpful, friendly visits during which the worker kept them up to date on the plans being made to secure Bonnie's release.

Bonnie had come to live with the Prousts in mid-May. In August, agency representatives were due in court to renew a conditional order placing the child in foster care. The biologic mother and her legal representative were supposed to attend this hearing. When neither appeared, the agency's counsel moved to have Bonnie freed for adoption on grounds of abandonment. The court surrendered the child.

Joseph and Donna Proust immediately had their attorney initiate adoption proceedings. The state in which the Prousts make their home requires a six months wait from placement of a child into an adoptive home until the adoption can be finalized. However, in cases where the child has been in foster care and is being adopted by these same foster parents, the court takes into account the foster care period during which the child and family were supervised by qualified social workers. Thus, six months after Bonnie came into their home as, first, a foster child and then an adoptive child, she became the adopted daughter of two by-then extremely doting parents.

"We invited her first foster parents to the party we

gave to celebrate the adoption," Donna recounted. "Bonnie had been their eleventh foster child and, had they been younger, they might have adopted her themselves. We wondered how she would greet them, if she would be confused by having two sets of parents in the same room. Bonnie hardly reacted to their presence. I was shocked, and hurt for them—after all, they'd cared for her the first two years of her life. If they were offended, they never mentioned it. They obviously were happy to see how Bonnie had grown and that she was well taken care of. I gained so much respect for them, good people who can love and care for a child and then have the strength to let that child go. . . . I often wonder, if everything hadn't worked out for us, could we . . ."

Fortunately, Donna need not complete the sentence.

Intercountry Adoption

In America, intercountry adoption most frequently has involved the intercontinental transport of orphaned and abandoned children to homes and adoptive families in the United States. World War II was followed by an influx of youngsters to the States from the devastated nations of Europe. As the theaters of war moved to the Far East, the faces of children without homes changed—from European to Korean, then Vietnamese, including those who combined the features of their Oriental mothers and Caucasian or Negro fathers.

While small numbers of infants continue to be channeled to this country from European and Central American nations, from Mexico and Colombia, from any place in which the tremendous pressure to locate adoptable babies will unearth them, the great number of children in other nations who need homes *now* are to be found in Korea and Vietnam. More Americans are responding to this need. This is the intercountry story of adoption today.

Just before the Korean War, in June 1950, 8,908 orphans were to be found in 116 institutions in Korea. Following the cease-fire, in July 1953, 53,963 children were listed at 440 institutions. Additionally, tens of thousands of children not accounted for in official records made their home in the streets. Not all these children were orphaned or abandoned. Some eventually were reunited with family members from whom they'd been separated during the war. Small numbers—mostly healthy male infants—were adopted by childless Korean families. The majority remained.

"Well-meaning" individuals and representatives of social welfare organizations came into Korea to take its children out to homes in more stable, more developed nations. This wholesale exportation often included children who were not free for adoption, exiling these children from relatives, even parents, forever. Memories of these abrasive separations remain strong in Korea, and have affected the attitudes toward intercountry adoption in such recently wasted nations as Vietnam and Bangladesh.

Among the first significant steps in the development of overseas adoption of Korean children was the establishment in Korea in 1953 of the Child Placement Service, which came under the Ministry of Health and Social Affairs. By 1955, Catholic Relief Service was active in arranging adoptions of Korean babies in nations other than Korea. About this time, Harry Holt, a by-now-legendary Oregon farmer, acting on his personal conviction that every child deserves a home of his own, simply went to Korea to make that goal a reality. Often criticized for bypassing accepted child-placement procedures, including careful study of prospective adoptive homes, Harry Holt placed some 3,000 children with families outside Korea within a few short years. A dedicated Christian, his major requirement was that applicants seeking to adopt be believers in Jesus Christ. Holt reasoned that a truly Christian home was, by definition, a good home in which to raise a child.

Although Harry Holt is no longer living, the program that today bears his name is both a continuation and expansion of his work. Licensed by the state of Oregon in 1962, the Holt Adoption Program now provides a full range of pre- and postadoptive services for residents of that state. It also may service directly residents of the state of New Jersey and of the republic of Korea. Among the significant changes in the Holt Program has been the restructuring of the adoptions procedure along more professionally accepted lines and the relaxation of its religious requirement. Holt now describes itself as "a Christian, nondenominational, nonsectarian organization."

Agencies throughout the United States and those in other nations that looked askance at Holt's early methods now work co-operatively with this agency, not only to fill requests that come to them for Korean children, but to encourage individuals interested in adoption to consider a Korean boy or girl. Certainly, a good many agencies report an increase in the number of requests for Oriental youngsters by families in America. Their representatives ascribe this interest to: (a) the shortage of white babies; (b) response to the devastation wrought by wars in which American troops were directly involved. Couples who have sought to adopt healthy Vietnamese youngsters have, until very recent months, found so much red tape involved in taking any child from this country—the Vietnamese Government was opposed to intercountry adoption—many turned their gaze to Korea as an alternate source of children.

Paula and Stuart Spelman took this route. After their two sons, Ezra and Harlin, were born, the Spelmans began to think about adding a third child to the family. Proponents of Population Zero, they mutually decided it would be wrong for them to conceive a third child. Adoption seemed a reasonable means toward a larger family.

Stuart's brother, Aaron, a conscientious objector to all

wars and a cause-involved bachelor, earlier had attempted to adopt a Vietnamese child and was turned down by every group he contacted. It's difficult for a single person to bring any child into the United States. U.S. immigration law is carefully worded to deal with an adopting *couple*. It states that the petition to admit a child to this country for purpose of later adoption must be filed by a married couple, one of whom is a United States citizen. A marriage certificate and proof of termination of any prior marriage is also required. While some unmarried individuals have managed to import children, they've generally been persons who've spent time in the child's country of origin (servicemen stationed abroad, for example), who have themselves selected a specific available child and who have waged strong campaigns (involving letters written to congressmen and senators to intercede in their behalf) aimed at making that adoption possible.

Stuart and Paula reasoned they could succeed where Aaron Spelman had failed. Married six years, their credentials included a stable marriage that had produced two healthy, happy children. They enjoyed the benefits of a good income. Stuart, at thirty-three, was a successful interior designer. In addition to their handsomely appointed modern home in Connecticut, Paula and Stuart owned a cottage in Nantucket where the family spent its summers. They could provide excellent character references as well.

Paula made a phone call to the New York office of International Social Service and was told, curtly, that Vietnamese children were hard to get—"impossible" was the word used. The Spelmans did not speak of adopting again for almost a year.

At that time, friends who'd adopted an American Indian boy encouraged them to do the same. "I don't *think* we were looking for an exotic baby," Stuart now says,

"although I'm not completely certain we weren't. We
spoke of taking a child who might not otherwise find a
home—but we didn't seriously consider an American
black, and we certainly were aware of the publicity given
their availability, nor am I convinced we were ready to
handle a handicapped child. When we did go to the
agency that had placed the Indian child with our friends,
the woman who became our caseworker, Mrs. Picora,
made such potentially weighty decisions easy for us."

First, the caseworker informed the Spelmans, the adoption of a young American Indian child no longer was possible at her agency. Local prejudices have always been a
factor in a child's adoption possibilities. Puerto Rican
youngsters are more easily placed out of the New York
area. For a long time there was difficulty in finding homes
for Mexican children in such border states as Texas and
California, while Eskimo babies weren't welcomed by Canadian families and Indian offspring found greater acceptance in Canada or in Eastern United States than in
the West. By the time the Spelmans approached the
agency, this situation had altered to the point where there
were sufficient homes in the West, near the reservations,
for young, healthy Indian children who were to be placed
for adoption.

Stuart went on, "Mrs. Picora made the idea of adopting
a handicapped child easy to negate. She reasoned that
the demands of our young sons—Ezra was then five; Harlin, three—would make it difficult for us to devote the
necessary time to a child needing special care. Additionally, I travel a good deal in my work. I specialize in de-
signing the interiors of schools and public institutions.
Even when I'm in town, it's not unusual for me to put in a
six-day week, so the burden would fall largely on Paula
who, even given the daily assistance of a housekeeper, was
really involved in the care of our children. We didn't
question Mrs. Picora's reasoning. She'd taken us off the

hook. She also told us that while her agency had made some transracial placements, it wouldn't participate in any adoption by a white couple of an all-black child. 'What about a Korean baby?' she asked."

Yes, the Spelmans decided, a Korean child would be fine. Paula then specified a girl child, and not—as all her friends surmised—because she already had two sons. A strong feminist, Paula felt the future would be bleak for an orphaned female raised outside a family situation in the Korean society, in which only male children were looked on as having value. Both the Spelmans wanted a child who'd be younger than their sons.

The interview process they then embarked on was not unlike that experienced by most couples who work through agencies. Over a period of several months, Paula and Stuart were interviewed jointly and individually. The caseworker stressed the dearth of information on the backgrounds of so many abandoned Korean children. Not only were the Spelmans unlikely to receive any information on the family medical history of a given child, they might learn nothing at all about the child's mother, father, circumstances of birth. How did they feel about this? Comfortable with the couple's acceptance of the idea of a child of another race, one who wouldn't resemble the other members of their family, Mrs. Picora asked them, "How do you feel about adopting a child who might not be an achiever?"

Paula began to wonder, "Were we sincere in wanting to adopt this third child? Were we role-playing—carrying the banner of the Eastern liberal?" She and Stuart put off their home study until September, to spend the summer thinking through the honesty of their motivation to adopt a Korean child.

At about this time their son Ezra, who'd been delighted with the idea of a Korean sister when the possibility first was raised, became adamantly opposed to the idea. He

feared his friends' ridicule. His parents chose to view this
rejection as symptomatic of a phase: overconcern about
peer group opinion. They decided not to let it affect their
plans to adopt. Having to deal with Ezra's doubts, however, helped them clarify their own feelings. They now
knew they sincerely wanted this third child.

In late September, when their home study had been
completed, Mrs. Picora forwarded the Spelmans' application to HAP (Holt Adoption Program) in Creswell, Oregon. Holt then set about finding a child for the couple.
Stuart and Paula later realized they could have made the
initial contact directly with Holt, who would have referred
them to a local agency for a home study afterward. In their
case, it made no difference which came first—the local
agency or Holt. Today, John Adams, executive director of
HAP, suggests Holt be contacted first. He explains the
change: "We are accepting a spot on the waiting list at
the point of beginning the application process rather than
accepting the applications as we were before and then
having people wait after the home studies are approved.
We have changed the procedure as the waiting time has
gotten longer and it is important that people write to us
now *in order to begin the process a couple of years from
now.*" This is the situation for people wanting infants and
young children, as did the Spelmans. The other side of the
coin, according to Mr. Adams, is that, "We need homes
more than ever before for . . . children of elementary
school age who have no chance of a home in Korea and
yet who are perfectly capable of still making reasonably
good adjustments here in the United States. . . ."

Even before a specific child was referred by Holt, the
Spelmans became busy gathering and filling out many of
the forms necessary to the legal procedure. They hired a
lawyer recommended by their local adoption agency to
guide them through these steps. They obtained certified
copies of their marriage certificate and of Stuart's birth

certificate, necessary to accompany Form I-600, which is filed with the U. S. Immigration and Naturalization Service, establishing the responsibility of the signer for the incoming child.

During this time, the Spelmans received quite a bit of mail from the Holt organization. Included with the routine forms on health and family background was a page asking the applicants to discuss when they first came to Christ. "I panicked," Stuart recalls. "We aren't Christian, and I suddenly had the feeling there'd been one gigantic mistake—we'd never be eligible for a baby through the Holt Program. Mrs. Picora calmed me down, assured me the policy had changed, and simply advised me to write 'Does Not Apply' across that page. I did, and we never ran into a problem."

Leftovers of their Thanksgiving dinner were still in the refrigerator when the Spelmans received a telephone call from Mrs. Picora. There was a little girl . . . full-blooded Korean . . . six months old . . . in an orphanage in Seoul . . . no known facts on parents . . . apparently in good health. She had a picture of the child, which she'd be pleased to show them.

The baby in the photograph, which shows signs of all the handling it has since received, bears little resemblance to the bright-faced, giggly little girl now known as Jordana who has become an integral, rather noisy member of the Spelman household. It is a blurred photo of an unsmiling, anonymous-appearing Korean baby, whose matted black hair failed to cover the blemishes spotted across her forehead. To Paula and Stuart, who rushed to the agency office to see the photograph, the child who was pictured immediately became *their* baby. From that moment, nothing could happen soon enough to suit Stuart.

"In our situation," he explains, "we weren't anxiously awaiting a baby in order to become parents. I guess that's why we really didn't feel the pressure of the passing of time as we underwent the lengthy adoption procedures. Once a baby was assigned to us, it all took on different meaning. Once we had a name and picture, the baby became a living, breathing creature. Suddenly that was *our* daughter crowded in with others in an orphanage in Korea, our child who was sitting up, perhaps learning to stand, probably in need of care. We wanted her home. I practically lived in the lawyer's outer office. Because he was occupied with other matters as well as with our adoption, I practically took the forms from his secretary's typewriter and literally walked them through the bureaucratic maze."

The child's legal papers (birth and release certificates) were sent from Korea. Back home, the local agency assembled proof of the Spelmans successfully having met the pre-adoption requirements of their state. Because Paula's and Stuart's fingerprints had to be sent to Washington, D.C., to be checked out by the FBI, the Spelmans went to their neighborhood police precinct to be fingerprinted. Paula's prints didn't come out well and had to be retaken, causing a two-week delay in the adoption process, which continues to rankle Stuart. He now tells others adopting a child from a foreign country, "Have your prints done at a local FBI office, an armory, at any appropriate federal agency, and be sure they do it well."

While the Spelmans and agencies acting in their behalf were thus busied in the States, the immigration officer in Korea verified that the little girl whose photograph was now cherished by the Spelmans was indeed the same child described in the legal papers, that she was actually available for adoption, had no physical defects not previously noted, and did not have active TB. After the child's Korean travel documents were secured and her visa approval came through, Holt arranged to include the little girl on a group flight of youngsters being escorted to adoptive families in the United States. There's generally a wait of from two to five weeks for this flight, sometimes longer.

As a rule, adoptive parents receive a letter from Holt containing information on their child's arrival date and hour. They're told to be at the airport at least an hour before flight time, but cautioned, "If you live a long distance from the airport, do not leave home early except if you are willing to do so at your own risk."

The Spelmans couldn't wait. On the day they were to meet Jordana's plane, they left for the half-hour trip to the airport at least two hours before the flight was scheduled to land, which was five in the evening. Had Paula and Stuart managed to contain their excitement, Ezra's enthusiasm alone would have dictated their leaving early. His parents had correctly assessed the boy's earlier opposition to the adoption. When news that he might become brother to a Korean sister leaked to his classmates, Ezra became an instant celebrity. Nobody else had a comparably exciting item to contribute. Now, Ezra could not wait for his baby sister to arrive. Harlin felt the tension, but really understood little.

The family visited the airport coffee shop. The children and their father climbed to the observation tower while their mother tried to guess which of the other couples in the lounge were waiting for children. At last, the airport clock read five. The plane was on schedule. The first passengers came down the ramp. Several were Oriental. None were children. Where was Mr. Kim of the Holt Agency and where were the children? No escort was evident. No children emerged. Typically, the children's flight had been rescheduled for three hours later.

Soon more parents arrived. Each family had a snapshot of an awaited child. Some had previously adopted Korean children. Excitement mounted. When the big plane landed, Mr. Kim and half a dozen boys and girls were on it. The older children were frightened. They clung to

their escort; some whimpered. The Spelmans, who knew
they were to receive the youngest baby, correctly reasoned the little girl in Mr. Kim's arms belonged to them.
They had to wait for her as, one by one, the names of the
adopting adults were called. Each had to sign a "receipt
for one child." Each was given a number of documents,
including a flight report and vaccination record. And
each was given his child.

"Then, just like that, we were free to go," Paula recalls.
"We went directly to our car, automatically began the
drive home and—somewhere along the highway—decided, 'Hey, let's stop and take a good look at her. This is
our daughter.'

"She was asleep, and so tiny. She weighed fifteen pounds
at nine months. When she awoke, probably because we
jostled her, she smiled. It seems she's been smiling ever
since. The day after her arrival, we took Jordana to our
pediatrician for a checkup. She had a bad case of diarrhea,
easily explained by the change in her diet if only on the
plane ride, which didn't help clear up a nasty-looking
diaper rash. Several abscesses on her head looked a lot
worse than they were, and she had sizable blue-black
spots on her buttocks, which, we were told, were Mon-
golian spots, common with Oriental babies. They aren't a
medical problem."

There *are* medical problems commonly found among
many of the children from Korea. Parents who adopt these
children ought to be aware of them so they can alert their
doctors to any condition that may require treatment. Often
it is wise to seek a doctor familiar with diseases of the
Orient, for there have been cases in which undetected
and unrecognized exotic parasites have seriously affected
the young people in whose bodies they lodged.

One active organization of adoptive parents of Oriental
children, OURS of Minneapolis, Minnesota, publishes an
excellent international adoption handbook that contains

much useful information, including a rundown of special medical problems. The most common of these fall under three categories: parasites (mainly roundworms); positive Mantoux (test for TB, which is prevalent in Korea); and head lice. The last is the least serious of the three, although lice can spread to other members of the family and must be treated. A positive reaction to a TB test may require treatment and checkups to prevent the germ from becoming active. Parasites are quite a common problem to the children who are old enough to be eating table foods, because human wastes frequently are used as fertilizer in many rural areas of Korea. Conditions in several orphanages were such that children sat around in their own, or others', fecal matter. OURS advises all adoptive parents of Oriental children to have their doctors check for parasites not just once but several times, since parasites have cycles and at times fail to show up in the stool specimen.

Jordana and her adoptive family are fortunate. Over-all, the little girl was in good health. Her skin has cleared. The bluish spots ought to disappear by the time she celebrates her fourth birthday. No longer small for her age—she might well be described as "plump"—she astounds her family, particularly her brothers, with the quantities and variety of food she manages to consume. The American diet poses no problems for her. Nor did she suffer any other difficulties in adjustment from one culture to another.

When Jordana's adoption was in process, Stuart and Paula had read Jan de Hartog's excellent book, *The Children,* in which the noted author speaks of his and his wife's experiences with their adopted Korean daughters and discusses general aspects of intercultural adoption. They learned that nightclothes were unfamiliar to many of these youngsters; indeed, a good number were more accustomed to sleeping on the floor, surrounded by other family members, than they were to beds in rooms of their own. Mr. de Hartog recommended placing a mattress on the floor if necessary, leaving the bedroom door ajar, a light on in the hall.

Jordana fell easily asleep in her new crib. Studies done on the adjustment of Korean adopted children have verified the obvious: children placed at an early age have fewer initial problems related to culture. It is the older child who has to deal with questions of insecurity, fear, rejection, and language barriers as well as hunger, fatigue, and dietary problems. It is the older child who will stay awake at night, remembering now-distant friends and places. It is the older child who is suddenly thrust from the security of the group, however insecure his personal situation, into a transnational and transracial situation that affects his social acceptance by the larger community and with which he alone must cope.

Daniel Port, whose mother was a Korean camp follower and whose father was an American Negro G.I., has been the adopted son of white, educated, affluent parents, Tracy and Lilyan Port, for more than ten years. At eighteen, he has not yet resolved his problems. A personable, bright boy who has nevertheless become a school dropout, Danny says he would like to be an architect. His mother believes he means it, too, but thinks he's unwilling to give up one moment of immediate pleasure to study for what may be tomorrow's rewards.

An articulate woman, Lilyan Port seems most insightful in explaining Danny's problem as a result of earlier influences on his life. "He's a gutsy kid," she says with affection. "He always has been. I don't recall having ever seen him cry. He gets angry, of course, but it's mostly directed at himself and it doesn't last long. He seems to shrug disappointment off quickly, probably too quickly. Danny hasn't spoken of Korea in years, so I'm just piecing bits of information together. When he first came to us and after he'd learned enough English to express himself so we could understand him, he used to speak of his mother and her many boy friends. She surrendered him when he was seven, in hopes he'd be adopted by an American couple and make a better life for himself. . . . I gather he lived from day to day in the camps. That seems to be his pattern today. He grabs at whatever is good *now*, without waiting for later, better gratification."

Looking back, his adoptive parents suspect they did something wrong, although they're not certain what it is. "Perhaps we shouldn't have been so indulgent," says his mother, "but for a long time after he arrived, Danny seemed so troubled—not when he knew he was being watched. Then you'd think he hadn't a care in the world. When he was off his guard, in his sleep, he cried out and tossed about. He didn't make friends easily—that's hard to remember, because now's he's always off somewhere with his friends—and so, when he turned into a bit of a clown and began to disrupt his classes, we were more relieved than disturbed. His teachers pushed him ahead, even though he hadn't completed his grade's work satisfactorily, and we let them do it, expecting him to straighten himself out one day."

"It's very easy to get out of blaming yourself when you adopt an older child," says Danny's tall, sun-tanned father. "The events of his earlier life afford you an escape hatch for when things go wrong later."

Tracy and Lilyan Port, who have a biological son older than Danny and now away at college, didn't know any couples who'd adopted a child from Korea when they decided to do so more than a decade ago. Moved by tales of the victims of the Korean conflict, they wrote to Pearl Buck, who referred them to International Social Service. Their circle of friends doesn't include others who've since made similar adoptions. "There just weren't any in our neighborhood," Lilyan Port explains. Danny has never been to a Korean restaurant in the United States. There are none in his community. He has no Korean friends, although he's well liked by the fellows in his sports club, all of whom are white. There are many girls among his friends, but he has never dated.

At age five, Tai O'Hare is too young to date. His adoptive parents, Kay and Sanford O'Hare, are less concerned about that eventual problem than they are about whether Tai will someday walk with crutches, open a door for himself, be able to carry his own books. Tai is a post-polio child from Vietnam.

Although the O'Hares live only a short distance from the Ports, the life-styles of these two couples are worlds apart. Where the Ports live well in an affluent community, the O'Hares occupy an old house along an unpaved street in an area that would never be featured in the front window of any real estate agent's place of business. The house is roomy and the O'Hares seem to live quite comfortably in a state of manageable disarray. The large back porch is filled with boxes, which in turn are filled with clothing, medical supplies, and toys that will be forwarded to a local branch of Friends of the Children of Vietnam and thence sent to orphanages in Vietnam.

Sanford and Kay O'Hare spend more time than seems possible working with the Friends, counseling men and women who seek to adopt Vietnamese children, lobbying for legislation to help the children who live in poverty and ill health in the overcrowded child-care institutions of Vietnam. In addition, the Friends plan many picnics and parties in their communities so that transracial and transnational youngsters can meet with others of similar background while their parents exchange information on discipline and dietary problems, support one another during times of stress as both adoptive parent and adopted child adjust to living together. Whereas Danny Port has no Korean friends, Tai O'Hare has many from Vietnam, Korea, and the Philippines. Where Danny's favorite snack is a cheeseburger, Tai is delighted when his mother serves *kim chee*, a popular dish in Vietnam. The adoptive mother of a Korean daughter gave the recipe for *kim chee* to Kay O'Hare, who has since passed it on to many another family with an Oriental child.

The O'Hares are devoted to Friends of the Children of Vietnam for many reasons, not the least of which is that this is the organization through which they located Tai. Adopting a child from Vietnam has been at best a long and tortuous project. Many who were moved to investigate such adoption found it an impossibility. When Sanford and Kay, newly wed and fresh out of college, came to International Social Service with their request for a Vietnamese child, they were told no . . . impossible . . . out of the question. The Vietnamese Government wasn't in favor of it. Those couples who did manage to adopt had to have been married more than ten years. They had to be childless. The O'Hares hadn't even tried to have a child "of their own." "No," said the man at International Social Service. During the next year, Sanford and Kay contacted, one after another, the recognized agencies that were successfully involved in placing children from Korea with American families: Holt; Welcome House in Doylestown, Pennsylvania; Lutheran Social Service of Minneapolis, Minnesota. The response was always the same: no.

For most couples, that would have been that. The O'Hares, however, were not to be put off. There are an estimated five hundred orphanages in Vietnam. Newspaper stories have told of these understaffed institutions, of overcrowded conditions, of children dying of malnutrition, parasites, a variety of diseases that could have been treated had adequate care been available. "Surely," says

Kay, "if so many Vietnamese children were dying, we could do something to save just one child."

A newspaper article is credited by the O'Hares with bringing that one child to their home. On the feature page of their local newspaper, the story had to do with relief work undertaken in Vietnam by an organization named Friends of the Children of Vietnam. After reading the article, Sanford wrote the Friends at their Colorado head-quarters and asked for advice on how to go about adopting a Vietnamese child.

It was an important contact. While adoption was a minor program of the Friends, their major emphasis being on helping the children of Vietnam in their native land, many members had adopted Vietnamese youngsters in-dependently—without going through an agency. This fre-quently involved their traveling to Vietnam, locating a specific child for adoption, then gathering a great many documents required by the governments of two countries, including the child's birth certificate (many abandoned children have no papers and no living relatives). In cases in which the adoptive parents did not meet Vietnamese requirements, it was often necessary to arrange for a spe-cial dispensation, which had to be signed personally by the President of South Vietnam.

Those who wished to adopt but who could not go to Vietnam (round trip fare to Saigon is about $1,200 per adult) were put in touch with individuals who knew of an available child. The next step for them was to locate a Vietnamese family willing to act as foster parents to the child while his papers were being prepared. An alarming number of the children were so weakened by malnutrition and illness that they did not make it to their waiting adoptive homes.

At about the time they received the letter from Sanford O'Hare, Friends of the Children had heard from an Ameri-can pediatrician stationed in Vietnam. He was looking for a family for a two-and-a-half-year-old boy of Vietnamese-Caucasian parentage who had been abandoned by his mother after polio left him permanently crippled. The boy, Tai, required special care that he was unlikely to come by in his native land.

The Friends asked Sanford and Kay if they could be interested in adopting Tai. "Of course we were," says Kay. "If we'd been looking for an easy route to parenthood, we wouldn't have come this far." But the road did not end here. Another fifteen months were to pass before Tai would arrive in the States. During this time, Tai was placed in foster care with a Vietnamese farmer and his wife. In the States, the O'Hares hired a lawyer recommended by Friends of the Children to assist them with the paper work. "You can save money," Kay advises, "if you indicate a willingness to do some of the work yourself. Even so, it cost us more than six hundred dollars, in fees and plane fare, to bring Tai into our home."

A wary child who'd been poked and prodded by so many strangers in his young life (How could he know they were doctors who sought to help him?), Tai was suspicious of every new character who had a role in the unfolding drama of his life. To put Tai at ease, Kay and Sanford tried out some basic words of Vietnamese, which they'd studied during the fifteen months they waited for their son. He was unresponsive. When they learned he would have to enter a hospital for surgery within weeks of his arrival, they got in touch with the Oriental Studies department of a nearby university, asked if any Vietnamese students were enrolled, and found several willing to spend some time visiting with Tai. The students explained hospital procedures to him, which helped allay some of his fears. The operations were completely paid for by the state in which Tai now lives. It is one of many in this country that have excellent programs to cover costs of medical care for their handicapped citizens.

"Sanford and I marveled at how well Tai came through his hospital experience," Kay recalls. "He's a survivor. He had to be to make it this far."

Now five years old, Tai remains uneasy around strangers if his mother isn't within touching distance. If he's standing, in his full hip-to-ankle braces, at the toy chest at one end of the family room, supporting himself by holding onto its wooden rim, he will suddenly drop to the floor and crawl to Kay, asking—in unaccented American English—that she join him in an activity or, right that minute, prepare a snack. Tai has developed a craving for chocolate chip cookies. Kay hugs him briefly, reassuringly, then matter-of-factly tells him she's busy at the moment and sends him on his way. That doesn't please her son. "Tai is at the stage, now," Kay says, "where he feels secure enough to be sassy. That's lovely. At first, whenever Sanford or I scolded him, he'd duck his head and pout—'to save face,' a typically Eastern reaction. Now he can act out once in a while, which indicates he feels secure."

Intercountry adoption proved the solution for this one child, Tai, from one nation, Vietnam, at one time in its history when, struggling with the multiple problems of a country at war, the nation was unable to care for its troubled children. There are signs that the South Vietnamese Government is relaxing its position on the adoption of some of its children. American agencies have been taking steps to establish regular procedures for such adoptions in co-operation with Vietnamese authorities. In March 1973, the Colorado chapter of Friends of the Children was licensed as an adoption agency and subsequently registered with the Vietnamese Ministry of Social Welfare. The Holt Adoption Program, which has its headquarters in Saigon, was licensed by the South Vietnamese Government in February. The Catholic Committee for Refugees of the United States Catholic Conference and the Travelers Aid-International Social Service of America (TAISSA) are also stepping up their adoption programs.

Following any disaster, natural or man-made, there will always be children in need of homes. Earthquake in Venezuela . . . war and famine in Bangladesh . . . children must be rescued from poverty, disease, and from death. Intercountry adoption is one answer. But intercountry adoption is not mass movements of children from one nation to another. It is not—and cannot be—a substitute for an adequate system of child care within any nation itself.

Recently, representatives of a well-known adoption agency in the eastern section of the United States were reported as having traveled to Sweden to place a handicapped black American boy with an adoptive family. The women visited the Adoptions Centrum, a private agency in Stockholm that acts as a referral service and clearinghouse for couples who've adopted or hope to do so. They brought with them pictures of other American handicapped children, black and white, whom they hoped to place with Swedish families. They claim homes cannot be found for these boys and girls in their native land.

It gives one pause.

Independent Adoption

Persons interested in adopting a newborn child generally have the option of working with established adoption agencies or locating an infant independently, on referral by a lawyer, a doctor, a religious leader, or another interested, involved third party. This legal, alternate means of bringing together an abandoned child with adoptive parents has had the unfortunate label "gray market" imposed on it by advocates of agency adoption. The title, which has stuck, infers illegality, a sense that there's got to be some hanky-panky going on somewhere. Does gray not have shadings of black?

There always have been black market dealings in children, situations in which infants are "sold" for large sums of money, in which legal procedures are bypassed and birth certificates falsified. As the supply of healthy infants diminishes, such horror stories increase. We deal here not with this black market—which must be recognized as one form of independent adoption—but with the vast gray market, which operates within the law.

In the past, many couples adopted privately because agency rules that insisted on religious matching, that set age limits for adoptive applicants, and that frowned on any previous marriage by one of the partners now seeking a child would have precluded their becoming parents. It was for them a necessary alternate plan.

One such couple were the Leighs, Penny and Ben, childless after thirteen years of marriage. The United States was enjoying a baby boom when the Leighs approached a well-known private agency to inquire into their chances of adopting. Penny was Catholic; Ben, Unitarian. They were told, "We have a lot of lovely babies. If the two of you will join a church and attend services for three months, then bring us a letter from your pastor, we'll be glad to do something for you." Penny decided that hypocrisy wasn't a good base on which to build a family. She and Ben let the word out—they were looking for a baby.

"You've got to let everyone know," Ben explained, "even though it seems a great invasion of your own privacy, because the unlikeliest people will lead you to the best sources." The Leighs received calls from wives of doctors ("My husband knows of someone who could help you. . . ."), from a law clerk who seemed nervous about a proposed meeting, eventually from someone who knew a doctor who, when contacted, referred them to an upstate lawyer who dealt forthrightly and honestly with the couple. Young John Benjamin Leigh is now eight years old.

Roger Permissant was fifty-one and the father of teen-age children by his first wife. Doris, his second wife, was thirty-eight when the Permissants became interested in adoption. Agency workers looked upon them, at best, as parents to an older child. Doris and Roger wanted an infant. The five-year-old little girl who has been their daughter since the week she was born was located via a doctor who then sent the couple to a lawyer he knew who handled the legal work for the family.

Still other men and women who could have met agency

standards with ease came to the gray market because of
stories they'd heard about agency procedures. Depend-
ing on the policy of an institution or the worker's psychological orientation, in many cases couples were made
to lay bare some of the most private details and emotions
of their lives. Some husbands and wives found this a degrading experience. Others believe the questioning added
to their self-knowledge and, eventually, made them better
marital partners and parents. A good many adoptive parents simply learned to play what, in adoption circles, is
referred to as The Interview Game, the basic rule of
which is: "Tell them what they want to hear." Those
who've been unwilling to play and have been able to pay
number among the persons for whom independent adoption has been the answer. Today, when a good many
agencies are not even taking applications for healthy infants, men and women on shakier financial ground but
who want newborn children are turning to the gray market. They are dismayed to learn that here, too, there are
fewer sources of babies, costs are spiraling, and there is
no guarantee that a couple will be able to find a baby.

Up to this time, what has it been like to adopt a baby
privately? While no two tales of independent adoption
are the same, similarities among cases emerge. Those
who have adopted with an attorney as intermediary will
recognize bits of their stories in the account of how Sheldon and Cora Adelman came to adopt their daughter
Janine, now six, who was followed by Gabrielle, four.
The history is told by Dr. Sheldon Adelman, an articulate young pediatrician who arranged to meet me in his
toy-filled, cheery office located in a small medical center
of an affluent suburban city.

"There comes a time in your marriage," he began,
"after you and your mate have been trying to conceive a
child without success, when you begin to face the fact
that you have problems. So you go to a doctor and, unless

there's something glaringly the matter with one or the other of you, you'll get a diagnosis in somewhat vague terms: 'It seems unlikely you'll conceive a child' or 'The odds are low. . . .' Something like that. We doctors dislike hopeless terminology, so you'll seldom hear a medical man say anyone is 'incapable of conceiving.'

"Then you must decide whether you're going to keep trying, against the odds, or consider artificial insemination—a real alternative if the fault lies with the husband. That wasn't so in our case. We decided on a more positive step: adoption. Cora and I had no doubt we wanted a family. I'm in a unique position to work closely with so many parents and their children, biologic and adopted, and I'm convinced the basic pleasure of being a parent is nurturing. I have no hang-ups about adopting, but I didn't realize it would be so difficult to get a baby. Cora and I were young (I was thirty-one, she was twenty-seven), healthy, well educated (Cora taught school before the children came into our lives), with a good marriage and the potential of a good income. Why should there be any problem about our adopting a child?

"We're also Jewish. In our city, there was one agency that handled the bulk of adoptions of Jewish children. State laws prohibited our adopting a child of another faith. Because of the scarcity of Jewish infants, that agency—even during the years preceding abortion reform when there were plenty of babies available—was faced with a problem the entire adoption world has come to know: more applicants than infants. We saw the social worker here as oriented to discouraging applicants, then willing to work with the diehards who simply wouldn't give up."

The Adelmans weren't turned away by staff members. However, they knew the adoption procedures here were drawn out over a long period. They also knew couples who'd been through six months to a year of being interviewed ("Have you sought psychiatric help about your inability to conceive?" was a favorite question) only to be sent a form letter of rejection. When they pressed to learn the reason, these couples were told they were too success-oriented in their careers and wouldn't have enough time to devote to a child. Concerned that this might be their fate, Sheldon and Cora started investigating out-of-state agencies that worked with Jewish children and parents. All had residency requirements. The Adelmans then heard of a home for unwed mothers, more than halfway across the country, willing to cross religious lines in placement. Cora sent them a letter of inquiry and received a reply: come on down.

Cora and Sheldon flew cross-country to visit the home and were taken on a tour of the impressive, well-maintained facilities. "They had to justify the fine fees they were going to charge, which would have been in the neighborhood of fifteen hundred dollars in our income bracket, a healthy amount in those days," Dr. Adelman commented. The tour was well planned, culminating in the nursery, its bassinets filled with newborns. "Yes," said Sheldon and Cora as one, at that moment extremely vulnerable to any plan that would net them a baby, "we want one. What do we have to do?"

The first requirement was to extend their stay so they could be interviewed, jointly and separately, to determine the stability of their marriage. Some time after they returned home, a representative of the home came to see them (and other families in their geographical area who'd applied to adopt a child through this institution) for what goes down on the books as a house visit.

Assured all was proceeding smoothly, Dr. and Mrs. Adelman gave up their one-bedroom apartment in the city and moved to a house they'd bought in the suburbs —in a good town in which to raise a family. They awaited their baby. Foolishly (in retrospect) Cora had spoken to

the social worker at the first agency they'd registered
with and let slip that she and Sheldon had made application at the second, distant agency and had hopes of receiving a child shortly. The caseworker didn't take this
news kindly. She effectively withdrew the Adelmans from
consideration at her agency.

Eight months later, after Cora had written a file full
of letters to the out-of-state home, its worker wrote to say,
"We may not be the right place for you. We'll get in
touch with you again at some future date." Don't call us,
we'll call you. Sheldon believes the agency underwent a
change in policy and no longer was willing to make placements across religious lines. Anguished, Cora cried the
entire week following that letter of inferred rejection.
Sheldon decided, "To hell with all this agency crap. We'll
find a baby independently."

How to go about this?

"Laymen think all members of the medical profession
are connected to some intricate network that's part of an
international black market dealing in babies," Sheldon
stated. "Well, I'm not. Neither are those among my friends
who are doctors. What's more, I have a great respect for
the law. I wouldn't jeopardize my life and career to get
involved in something illegal, not even for a personal
matter as important as this one was. But I do have pa-
tients whom I know were adopted children, so I asked
some of their parents how they'd come by their children.
The name of one lawyer was frequently mentioned, always followed by a comment on his honesty and genuine
concern for his clients. Cora and I made an appointment
to see him.

"Our first meeting was reassuring rather than interroga-
tory. While he asked us several questions about our lives
and our plans for any eventual child of ours, the lawyer
said he saw no reason for us *not* to adopt a baby. He out-
lined the procedure to be followed. He explained that

solicitation of a child from its natural mother is illegal. Since he knew of no then-pregnant woman looking for a family to adopt her expected child, his role in the proceedings would be restricted to handling the legal end of the adoption once a baby had been located for us. He'd give us a list with names and addresses of attorneys in various other parts of the country who had among their clients expectant mothers, generally referred to them by obstetricians the women were seeing in prenatal care and to whom they'd announced their intention of giving up the child when born. [Sources not named by the lawyer, but cited by others: abortion counselors; contacts on college campuses; friends of the unwed mother, some of whom have themselves surrendered children for adoption.] Cora and I were told to write several persons on the list, asking to be informed if and when they learned of the availability of an infant. We could have mentioned a sex preference, but we had none. We wanted a healthy baby.

"The basic arrangement is that these out-of-state attorneys advise you of a 'situation' of an unborn child who, when born, will be available for adoption, according to the mother's present thinking. The data reads something like this: 'Situation of Brenda B. Age seventeen. Completed high school. Five feet four inches. One hundred and nineteen pounds.' The girl's medical history is given. Information on her family may also be included. If the identity and facts on the natural father are known, they may be mentioned as part of the situation. Based on this information, we were to decide if we'd be interested in the infant, when born, and to so inform the out-of-state lawyer."

Cora and Sheldon wrote to lawyers in Texas, Florida, and California. These states, plus Arizona, are favored by young mothers waiting out their pregnancies. The young women seem to like the warm climate and the fact that the states have sizable transient populations. A girl logically could go to any for a "vacation," return home with a suntan as proof of her story. Besides, it's pleasanter to wait out the prenatal period lounging beside a pool than huddled next to a radiator.

Within three months, proposals were received from California and Texas. One of the situations seemed better than the others; it included facts on the child's father that were encouraging as to academic potential. The Adelmans committed themselves to cover this girl's obstetric expenses, including the cost of delivery and hospital bills, and to agree to adopt the newborn if the baby was born healthy. At the same time, the expectant mother was sent biographies of Sheldon and Cora, with all facts correct but their surnames excluded, for she had to consent to have her baby adopted by them. This is contrary to most agency procedures, where complete anonymity is the rule rather than the exception.

If the religion of the prospective adopters is different from the one with which the natural mother is affiliated (the case in this adoption) and the mother consents to adoption by the couple, she must sign a paper in which she cites her religion and the religion *in which she wants her child to be raised.* The language of the law in the states concerned with the Adelman adoption proceedings reads that the adopters must have the same religion as the child, not as the mother of the child. Thus the woman who gave birth to the little girl whom she then consented to have adopted by Sheldon and Cora stated that, while she was born Catholic, she no longer practiced her religion. She fully understood the adoptive parents were Jewish and she authorized and directed her child be raised in the Jewish faith.

Had she wished, she could have insisted on a Catholic home for the baby . . . or a home in which there were siblings . . . or pets . . . or a home in a rural community

. . . or in placing her child with a young couple or with a mature man and wife. Says New York adoption lawyer Terry Milburn, "When independent adoption is practiced ethically, it is the biological mother who places the child based on biographies of prospective adoptive parents sent to her. The attorney does the necessary legal work but *does not place the child.*"

When the little girl who is today Janine Adelman was born, Cora received the call she'd been waiting for. "Congratulations," said the out-of-state attorney. "You've just become the mother of a healthy baby daughter."

Cora screamed with joy, phoned Sheldon at the hospital, and the very next morning the two of them were on a plane to pick up their daughter. They went straight from airport to hospital, where they were met by their out-of-state counsel. He requested a check for $1,000, which he indicated would cover the hospital bill and doctors' fees. Dr. Adelman thought that was high, but admits, "I didn't ask any questions. It didn't seem too far out of line and I wanted my baby." Because he is a pediatrician, Sheldon was permitted to examine the infant. (Nonmedical persons may elect to have their baby seen by any doctor of their choice, even though the infant is checked by the staff doctor or one known to the lawyer or obstetrician who delivered the child.)

"Then we went into a cab, which took us right back to the airport, where we got a plane, which took us right back to our own city, where we were picked up by my in-laws, and suddenly we were home," says Sheldon. He stops pacing the length of the office; his face breaks out in a broad smile as he remembers the moment: "All of a sudden this problem that has weighed on you for years has disappeared and in its place is this lovely pink bundle. I can't tell you how good that feels."

What followed were legal formalities. A social worker was sent by the court to do a study of the family. Such studies are more cursory than investigative, as in the case of agency adoption. Since the baby is already *in* the home, the worker seeks to approve the situation, not to decide if the couple is worthy of parenthood. This difference in attitude can make for a pleasanter relationship between family and caseworker.

At this point the lawyer who first supplied Sheldon and Cora with the list of out-of-state attorneys stepped back into the picture. He filled out the papers necessary to complete the adoption. Six months later, at a final hearing held before a surrogate, the adoption papers were signed and sealed. A new birth certificate was issued for Janine, with date and place of birth unchanged but with the names of Cora and Sheldon Adelman in the spaces provided for "mother" and "father." The cost of the adoption of Janine ran between $600 to $800 to the first attorney, at least an equal amount to out-of-state counsel, plus the money for hospital and doctor bills and airfare, excluding previous flights taken to visit out-of-state agencies, a step the Adlemans need not have taken. One reputable attorney cites $2,500 to $3,500 as the minimum amount a couple must expect to spend today. This includes the bills of two lawyers, all medical bills (doctors and hospitalization), and maintenance, if any, for the mother. Where maintenance is covered, it must be reported to the court. Medical problems (including delivery of the child by Caesarean section and premature births) can raise the figure as can airfares if the mother elects to fly to a distant state to await, and deliver, her baby.

Two and a half years later, the Adelmans went through virtually the same ceremony when they adopted Gabrielle —in the same manner, but without the agonizing and additionally expensive runaround that had preceded the adoption of Janine. Sheldon's assessment of private adoption as it worked for his family: "It's a good thing.

It's legal, reasonable, accessible adoption and it's honest in a way that agency adoption often is not. It says, 'You want a child; we will find you a child who needs a home and parents.' That's really where it's at, isn't it?"

The present scarcity of babies has made its impact on this "reasonable" and "honest" procedure to the point where, frequently, it has become difficult to distinguish gray from black. Terry Milburn, one of New York's better known adoption lawyers and herself the adoptive mother of three children, finds that greater numbers of unwed mothers, aware of the value of their commodity, are asking to be paid for giving up their newborns. When she tells them she will not help them make a profit on the child, they sometimes make other contacts. And it is these contacts, frequently other attorneys, Miss Milburn believes, who are giving the general group of ethical lawyers specializing in adoption—some forty across the nation—a bad name.

Many would-be adopters who contacted Miss Milburn in the early months of 1973 were told there was a possibility of a two- to three-year wait for an infant. That same month, the New York *Times* reported there *were* babies available to couples who knew the right word: money. To prove this, the *Times* reporter and a male friend posed as wife and husband seeking to adopt an infant. Their initial phone call to a top New York adoption lawyer elicited the response that no appointments could be arranged before the end of March. The lawyer added that the adoption situation was grim: the couple probably would have to wait two years for a baby. After the "husband" indicated money was no object and inferred that a baby was needed to save this marriage (the kind of reason agency personnel and many others in the field find unacceptable), the couple was given an appointment for the following week. Two days after the phone conversation, but before the scheduled meeting, the attorney telephoned with news of a white American baby about to be born. The costs to be covered were $9,500 plus his own legal fee of $2,500.

"Unfortunately," said Miss Milburn when asked to comment on the above story reported in the article, "more and more of this sort of thing is happening today. The result is to let money decide who is entitled to a baby and to exclude persons of moderate means from parenthood. I don't play the game that way."

When the game is not played with cards stacked for the highest bidder, it is very much like the legal procedure described by Dr. Adelman. Terry Milburn will speak to clients much as a social worker deals with people who seek to adopt via her agency. She wants to know about the length of the marriage, how the husband and wife coped with problems that attend the inability to conceive (for despite general changes in the picture of the adoptive couple to include parents with bio-children as well as newlyweds committed to the concept of Population Zero, the man and woman who shop the gray market almost invariably fit the standard illustration: partners in a marriage that cannot produce its children biologically). Miss Milburn wants to know if either party is reticent about adoption and is just going along with the idea to please the other.

She is careful to make clear the law and the inherent pitfalls: within a given time, the natural parent can change his or her mind; the child can be born in imperfect health and the couple may lose money placed in escrow for medical expenses; the court may question the qualities of the adoptive home. As matters now stand in New York, the mother who has consented to give her child up for adoption has thirty days from the filing of the petition to adopt in which she can change her mind and demand the return of the baby. There is then a hearing to determine what is in the best interests of the child, with no paramount right of custody in either the biologic mother or the adoptive parent.

The legal requirement of six months during which the couple has custody of the baby in foster care and six months' wait from the filing of the petition until finalization of the adoption has been amended so that both time requirements can run concurrently. It is therefore possible for the baby to be legally adopted within six months of placement, sometimes in less time if circumstances warrant.

Terry Milburn also points out that persons who contract to adopt are responsible for medical and hospital bills of mother and child even if the baby is stillborn or is born with a handicap, although they are not committed to see through the adoption of the child with special needs. This is accomplished by having the applicants place money to cover the estimated costs of medical and hospital bills in escrow pending the birth of a specific baby for whom they are waiting. "At this point," the lawyer notes, "some families decide to go no further. When they quickly take the warnings as an out, I know what they're dealing with. It's their uncertainty about whether adoption is right for them. 'Go home and think about it,' I tell them. 'Make certain this is really what you want to do. If you decide to go ahead, call me.'"

On the other side of each situation is the biologic mother. "Remember," Miss Milburn emphasizes, "in independent adoption, the natural mother is not simply surrendering her child: she is consenting to place that child with a specific couple, generally one she has selected from several biographies of families willing to adopt her child. It's been my practice, when dealing with her, to ask if she'd like to meet with the adoptive parents. If she says yes, I do my best to arrange that. It hasn't seemed to hurt the adoption over the long run in any way."

Such openness is not the rule. For each couple interviewed for this report who met with the bio-mother or
with another member of the baby's family (one woman
recalled how the infant she was to adopt was placed in
her arms by the maternal grandfather, who said with
dignity, "I give you my grandson. Be good to him."),
there are many others who have only the name of the
child's mother. And there are those who located infants
via a network of persons operating on the fringe of legal
private adoption who tend to be as unreasonable about
their fees as they are furtive in their dealings. Many an
adoptive parent has been made to play the tender scene
of confrontation with one's child in the setting of some
out-of-the-way parking lot, where the infant is switched
from one car to another as money changes hands.

The situation has reached a point where even those
people who strongly favor nonagency adoption are align-
ing with advocates of all-agency adoption, so as to put
the "baby sellers" out of business. Such a situation exists
in Delaware and Connecticut, where only adoptions
through public or private agencies are allowed. But unless agencies relax their requirements and open their doors
to middle-aged persons, previously wed persons, and
those of any faith (or of none), unless they can be set up
so that arbitrary selection and exclusion ceases to take
place where the fate of families is concerned, nonagency
adoption must flourish. And as more wheeling and dealing takes place in the gray market, responsible professionals in independent adoption may be forced to other areas
of the law, leaving the field to the opportunists and the
parking lot attendants.

Anatomy of an Adoption That Failed

"I don't think I could have talked about this a year ago," said Dorothy Craben when I phoned, at the agency's suggestion, to ask if I might visit the Crabens and speak about Skip, the young boy they'd taken into their home for adoption and returned to the agency seven months later. "The pain was too fresh then. It still isn't easy. . . ."

People are delighted to be given the opportunity to recall the moments of joy that have filled their lives; books have been written with stories of successful adoption. Understandably, those families whose tales of adoption don't come complete with a happy ending are reluctant to relive their failures. Having come through the preliminary stages of decision-making (Shall we adopt?), being interviewed and accepted as potential parents, and—finally—having a child placed in their home, it is no small matter when the grand plan fails. Caseworkers, too, seem to hedge when the topic of adoption failure is brought up. Each returned child symbolizes an error in judgment, a match mis-made: this particular child was wrong for this particular family. The conscientious worker wonders, "Why didn't I intuit this *before* placement?"

In an article on this topic, "Adoption Failure: A Social

Work Postmortem," Alfred Kadushin and Frederick W. Seidl report, "The best available information is that 97.5 per cent of all adoptive placements succeed." That 2.5 per cent of failure stands as a challenge to parents and professionals, all the more so today when so many children for whom placement is sought are older or physically handicapped—youngsters bound to carry problems along with them as excess baggage.

"If any good can come of our discussing the events that led to our rejection of Skip, if others can learn from our story," said Jerome Craben, "Dorothy and I would be willing to talk with you."

Jerome Craben met me at the airport of the small New England town in which the Crabens make their home. Holding tightly to his hand was his five-year-old daughter, Phoebe. Jerome is white; Phoebe is black. She is adopted. I remembered the words of the director of the agency through which Skip had been placed: "This was a transracial placement, but that wasn't the reason the Crabens couldn't keep Skip."

We drove to the Crabens' neat clapboard home, set in a garden of rosebushes, with Jerome Craben pointing out the natural sights along the way. He is with the park service, a career he could not have anticipated during his college days when he majored in psychology, but one which drew his interest during his army years, when he was stationed out West. He is lean, tanned, with the look of a tennis player or of a man who spends a good deal of time out of doors. Dorothy, his wife, is an art teacher. She has been working in a youth center twice a week since Phoebe joined their family five years ago at the age of three weeks. The story of Phoebe's adoption is relatively uncomplicated.

"After we were married for six years," said Dorothy Craben, a soft-voiced, soft-skinned, smiling woman in her mid-thirties, "Jerome and I began to think maybe we were missing something by not having any children. Since we hadn't had any biologically up to then—"

"We weren't really trying, but we weren't consciously *not* attempting to have children," Jerome interjects.

"We decided to do some thinking about adoption," his wife continues without a pause. Phoebe is playing with a friend in the garden behind the Crabens' home. "We'd crossed paths with two families who had adopted. One had about eight children, of all colors, sizes, and conditions, biologic and adopted, and that home seemed so wonderfully alive, it made a great impression on me."

Jerome picked up the tale: "Without much planning, one day we contacted a local agency whose name we found by looking under 'Adoption—Agencies' in the phone book. It was a private agency and the only one listed. We didn't know there were public agencies as well. The man who answered told us to write them a letter, which would serve as a formal application. We sent the letter off, beginning a regular procedure which ultimately led to our being approved for adoption of a white infant. We specified that we wanted a baby girl because that was Dorothy's strong preference.

"Somewhere along the way, however, we started thinking about a black child. We like to think of ourselves as intellectuals and we knew that black babies were having trouble being adopted. We'd met some couples who'd adopted transracially, but they seemed to be far-out do-gooders, and we're really rather conservative. Then we met other, more normal types—quieter people who didn't see themselves as trailblazers—who seemed to be successfully bringing up children not of their race. We thought we could do it, and told the agency.

"That inaugurated a series of additional meetings—to talk through our prejudices and our expectations—and finally we got this incredible little girl, Phoebe."

"I've never been so happy in my whole life as I was during the year that followed Phoebe's arrival," says Dorothy. "We ought to tell you this was in spite of the most awful reactions on the part of both our families. They live across the country, so their attacks came long distance, but they couldn't have hurt us any more deeply had they been launched at close range.

"When we first wrote them we were planning to adopt, Jerome's parents responded so joyfully, it increased our enthusiasm. My parents' reaction was more like, 'It's your life. We wish you luck.' In the next set of letters, we mentioned that the baby would be black. To put it mildly, the roof caved in."

Despite bigoted statements and ultimatums ("If you go through with this, we never want to see you again."), the Crabens sent infrequent letters to their respective families, often enclosing pictures of their daughter. When they planned a trip "back home," where they'd be staying with friends, they wrote and told their families they would be in the neighborhood. The families came, slowly, and were won over by the outgoing little girl. Now it is they who travel to New England. "More to see Phoebe than to spend time with us," says Dorothy.

By the time Phoebe had reached her second birthday, the Crabens decided it was time to expand their family. Dorothy wanted another daughter, but the adoption world was changing and infants of any race were in short supply. "When we went back to the agency, they told us, in pretty much these terms, they had nothing in stock," says Dorothy. "Jerome and I talked for a while and decided we could take a girl who was a bit older than Phoebe, someone out of diapers, perhaps a four year old."

The Crabens had become active members of an adoptive parents organization; thus the adoption grapevine knew they were ready for another child. One day Dorothy received a phone call from a social worker at a public agency. "I know you want a little girl," said the man, "but I have a seven-year-old boy who needs help right away." The boy, Stanley (who more readily answered to his nickname, Skip), was in a hospital where he'd been taken for treatment of wounds inflicted as a result of child abuse in his most recent placement (which had been intended to work into an adoptive home). He'd lived in two foster homes before that. Although he'd recovered and his scars were healed, Skip could not leave the hospital, for he had no place to go.

In retrospect, and trying to understand where the failures lay, Dorothy remarks, "We said yes, which may have been our first mistake: responding to an emotional appeal instead of being truly committed to parent a seven-year-old boy."

Following two brief visits to Skip in the hospital, where he had all the nurses at his beck and call, the Crabens admitted the boy to their home. "Can I say we welcomed him?" Jerome asks rhetorically. "I thought so at the time. Now I'm not so sure." Into the quiet, well-ordered lives of Jerome, Dorothy, and Phoebe came a whirlwind of a boy—handsome, strong, athletic, outgoing, extroverted, moody, seemingly independent, and *loud*. "I was jealous of him, maybe, I don't know," Jerome mutters, with a faint shrug of his shoulders.

"Skip was the biggest and the best," recalls Dorothy. "That was the image he had to hold of himself—only I wished he didn't feel a need to prove himself in every situation. Even at the dinner table, he had to have the first helping and the last, to eat the most, and the most quickly.

"With his contemporaries, he was a fanatic dictator. When I was working in the kitchen, I would hear him shouting orders to a group he'd had follow him into the garden. I don't know why the children put up with him, but they did. I suppose I could have seen in him a leader of men, but I only saw him as a boss. I was revulsed by his manner."

It wasn't long before complaints about Skip came home from school. He was disruptive; he couldn't sit still; he beat up other kids; finally—he was unmanageable. "Either Stanley goes," a harassed principal told the Crabens, "or I lose my teacher." A compromise plan was offered. "We'll keep Stanley till lunchtime," said the principal. "After that, he's yours."

"In a way, those afternoons may have been the best time we spent together," Dorothy now feels. "I'd make Skip sit at the kitchen table, doing the classwork he was missing by not being *in* class, while I knitted and did needlepoint. It's true, I had to constantly goad him to complete his work, but I felt we were becoming a possible family. After a few weeks of the togetherness, however, I'd had it. The good moments were few. It was the school's responsibility to handle its students, I decided, and I demanded they reinstate Skip as a full-time student."

The problems that arose in connection with school didn't help matters. They offered a focal point for a more general sense of dissatisfaction that the Crabens were trying to hold beneath the surface.

"To be perfectly honest," says Jerome, "I do believe there were those in the school who were critical of Skip because he was black—it's practically a lily-white school —so the transracial aspect of this adoption must be considered as a factor in its failure. Additionally, complaints came up before I got to know the boy. I never did, in fact. I tried to get close to Skip, but he wouldn't let me, so I couldn't make a judgment on whether the principal's grievances were well founded or if Skip was being maligned. I mean, if someone came to me and told me Phoebe was causing trouble, lying, or hitting other children, I might say, 'That's not like the child. There's got to be more to this story,' because I know Phoebe. But how could I know the arguments against Skip's behavior weren't justified?

"We'd never seen Skip hit a child; he was wonderful with Phoebe, who looked up to him without his having to do anything to earn her adoration and who followed him around the house like a puppy, but he did do some vicious things to our animals. [The Crabens have two dogs and an aging guinea pig.] And he was quite—purposefully—destructive, not of our belongings but of his own possessions. He systematically destroyed all toys that had been given him in affection and all mementos of his past. It's easy to play psychologist from a distance, and to find all kinds of explanations for these acts, but that doesn't take away from the fact they can be quite disturbing when you deal with them on a daily basis."

"That really was one of the problems," says Dorothy. "We had to work at a relationship with Skip twenty-four hours a day, seven days a week. It made me tense as a person and it led to so many arguments between Jerome and me, our marriage was threatened."

The more Dorothy found fault with the boy, the more Jerome decided his position had to be to defend Skip. In a dispute over rules, which were always changing as the Crabens tried to find their way in deciding what was appropriate for a seven year old (Should he be expected to make his bed? Take his own bath? Should he be permitted to cross two streets by himself to visit a friend?), Jerome always sided with Skip against Dorothy. Each parent was adamant on where he stood, yet—if pressured to explain his stand—each would have to admit his posture was insecure. "The minute Skip realized we were wavering," said Dorothy, "we lost ground. He did as he pleased."

During these difficult days, more and more the Crabens asked for counseling. It was not forthcoming. They spoke to their caseworker, who buoyed them with, "Hang in there." They consulted other parents who'd adopted older children; everything was fine, according to these other couples. Surely, then, thought Jerome and Dorothy, our case is unique. There must be something wrong with Skip.

"Later," says Dorothy, "after we both began to face up to the fact that the problem of Skip might be too great for us to cope with *ever* and we started baring our dirty laundry, these other couples began to open up and tell us some of the frustrating and difficult situations they were living through. By then it was too late. In our hearts, we knew Skip could not remain with us. But if those same families had been honest with us at the start, perhaps we could have seen our difficulties as an expected phase of a long, and ultimately successful, adjustment program. I don't know. I do know that, as we saw it, everyone else was doing fine and we were cracking up."

At the Crabens' request, the school psychologist observed Skip. She concluded the boy was hyperactive and recommended drugs to calm him down. A telephone to an analyst in private practice came up with the same recommendation. "Over the telephone," says Jerome indignantly, "and he hadn't even seen Skip!" No drugs were administered to Skip. The Crabens did, finally, have the boy seen by a staff of doctors at a renowned mental health clinic in a distant community. Their findings were that Skip was healthy, alert, *not* hyperactive. He was a deeply troubled boy who distrusted women (the person who'd punished him in his previous placement had been a woman) more than men, but who had learned to expect little from any adult. He needed security, love, and patience.

This analysis of Skip and his problems put into words something the Crabens knew had to be right, but by this time so much hostility had built up in them—plainly, they just didn't like the boy—that they doubted they could summon the patience needed to build a foundation for love.

Dorothy says, "Skip needed help. We all needed help. We asked for help. A clinic was being set up in our city, we were told. It wasn't ready to receive customers."

"During the early months of Skip's stay with us, I was working on a large project," Jerome recalls, "and so the hours I spent at home were few. That's probably why I was more hopeful that things would work out than was Dorothy. The social worker came out once a month, always on a Friday, and Dorothy would tell her we had real problems and she'd say, 'Hang in there,' and I'd come away feeling we could handle this, everything would be all right. Then I began to spend full weekends at home, and Skip got to me. How can I bring up small incidents and have you understand how large they grew in our lives? For example, I'd tell Skip he had a half hour before bedtime. There were five toys on his bedroom floor. If he cleaned up his room, I'd say, he could sit with me and I'd read to him. That boy would take the entire half hour to pick up the few toys, and then there'd be no reading time because, I think, he really didn't want it. I was hurt. And sometimes I was angry because Skip took so much of my time and energy, I realized I hadn't spent any good moments with Phoebe. There were times, after an episode with Skip, when I would walk into Phoebe's room, pick up the sleeping little girl, and cradle her in my arms. I needed the solace provided by the warmth of a child.

"At any rate, every Sunday night like clockwork we would have the 'Jerome Craben Hysterical Hour' in our home, after which I'd pick up the phone and try to get in touch with the caseworker. Of course, it being Sunday night, there was no way to reach her. Then she'd come round on a Friday, following a week when I'd spent most of my time at work, and I'd agree, yes, maybe we could hang in there, yes, maybe it would all work out.

"Finally, I knew I would have to choose between Dorothy and Skip. I realized I had more ties to Dorothy. As soon as I sided with her, I felt relaxed. This was more natural. But from then on, it was all downhill with Skip."

Once again, the Crabens asked for counseling. By this time, the local clinic had opened its doors. Promises of assistance came wrapped in conditions and tied with an ultimatum: yes, Skip needed help. Yes, the Crabens needed someone to speak with—a neutral, nonjudgmental outsider who could listen to them and suggest weekly programs of behavior modification, both for them and for Skip. There might have been something concrete to act on. They might have been able to go on. . . . But, said the clinic director, the staff would work with the family only if the Crabens guaranteed they'd see through the adoption. Skip needed that kind of commitment, said the director.

"They didn't know it," says Jerome, "but that was the straw that broke the camel's back. We had so many doubts, the only answer we could give was 'no,' because 'yes' was too risky. And so there was no help for us."

Jerome called the caseworker and announced this was it, they'd tried, Skip had to go. And right away, that week, no later. Skip overheard the conversation.

"Am I leaving?" he asked Jerome.

"Yes," answered Jerome. "We've learned that we cannot be the family you need."

"Do you like me?" asked Skip.

"You're all right," answered Jerome.

Skip seemed calm. He had learned to expect little from others. "And we proved him right," says Dorothy.

"Where will I go next?" Skip asked.

"I don't know," Jerome answered.

The night before he left their home, Skip cried. "I'm

gonna miss my friends," he sobbed. Jerome sat with the boy until he fell off to sleep.

The next morning, Jerome and Dorothy took Skip back to the agency. They've asked about him from time to time and have been told he was well. They believe he is once again in foster care. Skip is older now. It is unlikely he will find a family of his own.

"It's strange," says Dorothy. "When Skip left, I was exhilarated. I didn't look back. Yet, I'm amazed at how frequently I think of him. Christmas and his birthday are particularly difficult times to get through. I feel there was a death in our family a year and a half ago, and we will never completely recover from our loss."

Jerome, who up till now has been quite straightforward in recounting the story of Skip, gets up quickly from the lounge chair set in a clearing among the roses. He strides to where Phoebe has been playing, stoops, and cuddles the little girl, who sprinkles him with her watering can.

He returns to where we are sitting.

"It wasn't a brave decision," he says. "It was reality. Our marriage was at stake; our whole sanity was at stake. But there are times, when I look at photographs of Skip, that I think we could have made it. . . . We tried. . . . It just didn't work out. And we're really not sure why."

X In the Public Eye

As the preceding chapters illustrate, adoption has come out of the closet. Where secrecy, whisper, and innuendo often would surround the adoptive family in the past (because adoption carried with it the "stigma" of illegitimacy for the child and infertility for the adopting parent), openness is now more the rule than the exception.

This may have come about in part as a result of the increase in the number of older child adoptions, which call for a good deal of honesty. Not only the child involved but the greater community is well aware of his adoptive status. At the same time, the growth of transracial and transcountry adoptions created many families where children are visibly different from their parents, brothers, and sisters. Or perhaps a climate in favor of adoption as a means of family formation made it easier for adoptive families to come out in the open. In the public eye, they were recognized by others who began to ask, "What has it been like for you and for your child?"

Individual families organized with others into groups, at first to provide emotional support for one another when such questions arose, then to aid the newcomer to adoption by passing on knowledge gained through the experi-

ences of those who'd been there before. Many of these
parent groups expanded their activities to include educa-
tional and referral services to individuals who expressed
interest in adopting and to those who'd been rejected at
one agency and didn't know where next to turn.

One influential and effective citizens group, the Council
on Adoptable Children, was founded in Michigan (and has
since branched out across the country) as a direct result of
a series of rejections. More than a decade has passed since
Peter and Joyce Forsythe of Ann Arbor decided to adopt
a child who would not easily find a home. A handsome
young couple, the Forsythes were rejected by twenty-two
workers in several agencies during the course of four
years. The reason: they could have "their own" children.
Additionally, many caseworkers, responding to their own
biases in favor of the healthy white infant, thought there
must be something wrong with a couple who sought out a
child that didn't adhere to this norm.

After they finally succeeded in adopting Jimmy, who
joined their bio-children, David and Linda, and was followed by Martha and Paul (adopted), the Forsythes organized with half a dozen families who'd adopted youngsters
and who discovered they had something else in common:
a concern for *all* unplaced children and a desire to support
and foster programs designed to locate adoptive homes
for available children.

It was a logical step for COAC and many other organizations of concerned citizens to gather facts on children
needing placement and to pass this information on to persons who contemplated adopting a child. Association
newsletters often included photographs and short biographies of boys and girls for whom homes could not easily
be located. Some of these publications found their way to
similar organizations in other parts of the country, inspir-
ing inquiries for several of the youngsters whose biographies had been featured.

Nor have these groups confined their roles to servicing adoptive parents. Most have grown beyond the parent stage to include as members all persons interested in the welfare of children. The importance of these citizens organizations in bringing about many changes in the adoption world cannot be overstressed. Staffed largely by zealous volunteers, the organizations have, at the least, prodded the adoptive establishment to greater action on behalf of many children. On a larger scale, Michigan's Council on Adoptable Children (the same one founded by the Forsythes) was directly responsible for the establishment of Spaulding for Children, the agency whose sole purpose is the placement of the child who has not been easy to place. Members of New York's Adoptive Parents Committee successfully lobbied for passage of a twenty-four months' review bill, which requires that records of all children in foster care be reviewed every two years.

It is concerned citizens such as these who write congressmen whenever a bill having to do with the welfare of children is introduced, who not only pressure to have laws passed but who often initiate legislation. Having "gone public," adoptive parents and their allies are determined to go beyond their individual families to help all children who wait and the parents who wait for them. Local citizens groups (see Appendix for a list of these adoptive organizations) are excellent sources of information on respective agencies operating in their communities.

Many of the agencies, too, were aware of the need to reach larger segments of the public with information on homeless children. In this direction, they co-operated to establish state resource exchanges, which match rosters of waiting children with lists of adoptive applicants. The most far-reaching of these is the previously cited Adoption Resource Exchange of North America. With 723 participating agencies, this exchange makes the formerly isolated adoption agencies of North America part of a huge network of adoption resources. Through ARENA, two waiting sisters—one normal, one dwarf—found homes across the country with a family made up of a normal father, dwarf mother, plus two biological children: one normal height, one dwarf. "When you can get this incredible kind of situation, where you can place sisters in one household and assure that each will feel comfortable in her adoptive home, a situation which could only come about because of the large audience we reach," says Arlene Nash, ARENA's director, "you're encouraged to believe there is no child for whom you could not find a home if the network was expanded to include every agency and parent group in North America. Nor should our exchange be looked to solely for placement of severely handicapped children and of family groups, ARENA should be the unique resource for placing children—Oriental, Indian, black, Puerto Rican—within their own ethnic backgrounds."

While ARENA was a significant breakthrough, expanding the number of potential adoptive homes beyond the files of a single adoption agency, it won easy acceptance by many professionals, including some of the most conservative social workers, because it continued to respect the time-worn practice of confidentiality to a large degree.

One of ARENA's effective tools has been the distribution of a monthly newsletter that pictures a number of children who have been freed for adoption but for whom no family has come forward. ARENA discovered, as had those citizens groups that also included photographs of children in their literature, that persons who had expressed interest in one type of child frequently would be swayed to accept a youngster of a different age and sex from what they had specified. Applicants for healthy children would come forward to adopt handicapped youngsters once they found themselves drawn to a particular picture or biography.

This discovery developed into a growing trend across the United States toward the increased use not only of newsletters but of books filled with pictures of all available children for scrutiny by all parties interested. The picture books are sponsored and maintained by both citizens groups and local governmental agencies. They are distributed by subscription to adoption agencies and lay organizations, and they are successful. The Illinois Child Care Association has reported that, during their book's first year of use, 272 of 278 children pictured found homes.

The picture books are but another form of resource exchange. While highly visible, they too manage to operate behind a kind of one-way mirror, safe from the prying eyes of the greater community of those persons who are in no way involved in the world of adoption.

That curtain of secrecy was ripped away by other, more dramatic means of publicizing children waiting for families: use of the media. In spring of 1964, the Deputy Minister of Welfare of Ontario, Canada, approached the managing editor of the Toronto *Telegram* with a problem: what could be done about bringing to the attention of the public the difficulty in finding homes for handicapped, interracial, and older children whose prospects of being adopted were dim? Reporter Helen Allen joined the brainstorming session out of which came the idea for a three-week series on adoption. As part of the series, a picture was run of a fifteen-month-old girl of mixed race. In those days, the little girl was hard to place because of her black heritage and because she fit the then-definition of an older child. Within a week, forty letters were received from readers interested in adopting the child. One told how "my wife and I sat up three nights with this child's picture in front of us and then we decided to write for her."

Clearly, newspaper publicity had been effective in creating a response to a particular child. Just as clearly,

visibility was an important factor. Had the little girl been
described but not pictured, the results would have been
less encouraging. Future articles, run with and without
photographs, bore this out. The *Telegram* received ninety
letters from the three-week series and parents were found
for eighteen children, among them a family of Indian
children, girls ten and five, and their eight-year-old
brother.

The series led to a column, "Today's Child," in which a
hard-to-place youngster, or sibling groups referred by one
of the branches of Ontario's Children's Aid Society, was
featured daily. Several local branches refused to co-oper-
ate. They had no doubt youngsters would be placed, but
raised objections to invading a child's privacy. How
would such publicity affect the child not spoken for?
Would rejection not be one more—unnecessary, they
added—blow to a boy or girl already buffeted about by
society? Was it right to offer children as if they were merchandise?

Miss Allen's answer was that where more tactful placement efforts failed, hard-sell methods were worth trying.
That she was right is attested to by the more than 6,000
adoptions made to date as a result of her column, which
now appears in twenty-three newspapers and has attracted millions of devoted readers. Today Director of
Public Relations, Child Welfare Branch, Ministry of Community and Social Services, Toronto, Canada, Miss Allen
suggested and encouraged CFTO–TV, Toronto, to begin
"The Family Finder," a televised expansion of the newspaper column. "Buoyed by the placement of two children
with cystic fibrosis who appeared on the show, we are
planning one program entirely devoted to children suffer-
ing from this illness. We anticipate success," she told the
audience at a seminar on "Recruiting Parents Through
Media Presentation of Children," co-sponsored by New
York City Special Services for Children and an active cit-

izens group, the New York Council on Adoptable Children, and held in New York in January 1973.

Also on the panel was Ruth Carlton, women's metro editor of the Detroit *News*, who has been doing stories on the needs of available children since 1961. That first series brought a response of 2,600 letters from a public she awakened to the availability of older children for adoption (incidentally creating an awareness within social agencies that there were persons interested in non-infant adoption). Yet workers in many of these same agencies were leery of the weekly column, "A Child Is Waiting," which Miss Carlton inaugurated in August 1968. It features a photograph of a child (or family of children) waiting for adoption and a short descriptive piece about those in the snapshot. A box gives information on the number of families that asked for the child featured the previous Sunday. "Just like selling puppies" was the phrase commonly employed in complaint. If so, these were the puppies nobody went into the store to buy until Ruth Carlton shone the spotlight on them.

The children are the so-called hard-to-place. In all, 175 have found homes directly through the column in four years. Brothers and sisters are used repeatedly. A family of five adopted together is the largest group placed to date. Homes have been found for a ten-year-old girl ready to leave a mental hospital, a black infant with cerebral palsy, a ten-year-old deaf boy. Of the children placed in 1972, a sixteen-year-old white boy was the oldest. "It is imperative that the social worker really prepare the older child for adoption before his picture is made," says Ruth Carlton with compassion. "I suggest the approach: 'You were chosen to represent lots of kids who need homes . . . because you are such a fine boy. . . .'"

"I suspect those concerned about the side effects of a child's picture being used in newspaper adoption recruitment have either not experienced or have not placed in perspective the frantic searchings of a fifteen year old who has spent a lifetime in temporary foster care," wrote Wayne Anderson to Miss Carlton. Mr. Anderson is Director, Foster Care Service, Office of Youth Services for the State of Michigan. He went on, "I have repeatedly seen foster placements of several years' duration explode into a series of unsuccessful, very short-term placements brought about by a child frantically searching for who he is. I have little difficulty accepting the *very remote* possibility that a child might experience some temporary embarrassment over his picture being used in the paper. When I balance it against the proven results of using pictures, embarrassment can be overcome. The effect of a childhood without a permanent family cannot."

This point of view is gaining popularity. "At first I called around to the agencies to get a child for each week's column," says Ruth Carlton. "Now the agencies call me and I have a waiting list."

The same month that saw the start of Ruth Carlton's column—August 1968—also marked the beginning of a successful television campaign to place "special-needs children" in Los Angeles. Faced with growing numbers of these youngsters who were free for adoption but were not being placed, the Los Angeles County Department of Adoptions approached KTTV for free air time to tell the public of their plight and try to encourage some members of the audience to consider adopting this type of child. When Ben Hunter, host of a popular daily afternoon program of movies interrupted by many, many commercials, was approached ("Get Ben Hunter," someone is reported as having said. "He can sell anything."), he suggested having some of the youngsters actually appear on the show in addition to the adult who would discuss the adoption situation. It was to have been a one-time-only presentation. Audience response was so great, however, a decision was made to continue the program indefinitely as a regular feature. What followed is told in Mr. Hunter's words:

"In those days there was no danger of psychological damage to the children because they were all babies and were not aware of what was going on.

"Initially there was some concern that the county would be criticized for 'putting children on the auction block' (a term objectors love to use). The 'auction block' objection evaporated when they observed the manner in which we conducted the program.

"Four or five . . . babies were on stage, each seated on the lap of his social worker. As the camera took close-up shots of each child, I introduced him by a fictitious name, assigned for the purposes of the program. Then the camera turned to me and I explained that these children were being presented on TV because they are 'hard to place.' I then explained the county's adoption procedures. I explained that if you were interested in adopting one of these children you should telephone the county (we flash the number of the county on the screen during the entire program). After you call, the social worker will make an appointment with you and you can discuss it further. The period of time consumed in *very thoroughly* checking out the potential adoptive parents is described on the air as 'a getting acquainted period. Usually about six months.'

"After the explanatory remarks, the camera (and I) would return to each child and his social worker. As the camera would focus on each child, the worker would be interviewed about the child by me. At this time we would frankly discuss whatever problems the child has that made him a special-needs child. His problem might be medical or mental. Deaf and blind children have been adopted off the show, as well as children with myriad other ailments. Or he might be perfectly healthy, but 'special needs' because of his ethnic background. . . ."

The television show was so successful, both in finding

homes for the babies shown and in developing a public receptive to consideration of these youngsters, few babies awaited placement more than one year later. The decision then was made to include older children. By and large, the babies hadn't understood they were being discussed by Ben Hunter and the caseworker. Many weren't even aware they were being televised. Clearly this would not be the case with the older child.

New methods were adapted to this new situation. During the host's opening remarks and the following discussion of individual children, the youngsters are kept in a holding room out of earshot and without a TV monitor. They then come onstage, where they talk with Mr. Hunter about hobbies or anything else that seems to come up—not about adoption. A light tone is kept throughout this segment.

"Of course there's more to it than that," Ben Hunter explains. "These children know they are going to be on television. And they know why. It has been discussed with them very frankly by their social worker either singly or—when needed—in group therapy. None has gone on television against his will. Each child appears because he *wants to volunteer*."

The results are impressive—better than 90 per cent of the children have been placed as a result of the use of television. In actual numbers, that's over six hundred children.

Impressed with this kind of success, numerous stations across the continent introduced similar programs, from "Family Finder" in Toronto . . . to "Adopt-a-Child" in Dayton . . . to Dallas's "All You Need Is Love." While some of these no longer are in existence, similar shows are in the planning stage.

"The case for using the media in adoption," summarizes Leslie J. Roberts, executive director of the Children's Aid Society of Detroit, "is simply that it works!"

Children of Adoption

Our look at the world of adoption has thus far explored its variety, the decisions would-be parents must face up to before and during the process (Should we adopt? If yes, what kind of child can we parent?), the means of obtaining a child (whether via an agency or through independent channels), and the adjustment of the family members as recounted by the adoptive parents or by the agency caseworker, who sits further removed from the day-to-day living situation and generally loses track of the family once the first year following placement has passed. What has been missing are the voices of the children. It is all well and good to understand the process. The final question remains: *Does it work?* For this answer, we must turn to the adoptees.

This is a most difficult task, for most adults who were adopted as children remain undistinguishable from the rest of society. How to ferret them out? Just such a problem was faced by Benson Jaffee, associate professor of social work, University of Washington, Seattle, and Professor David Fanshel of the Columbia University School of Social Work, when they embarked on a study that was ultimately published under the title *How They Fared in*

Adoption. "Little is known about the degree to which adoption results in a satisfactory family experience," wrote the authors in the book's introduction, explaining the need for a work such as theirs, which reports the results of interviews with a hundred families who adopted children during the years 1931–40 through four social agencies in New York City. What the reader soon learns is that the study encompassed a series of interviews with the adoptive *parents* of the children, not with the adoptees themselves. The authors state that, although their original intent had been to use the adoptees as the primary source of information and to secure their perceptions of the adoption experience as their principal data, "it soon became apparent that this was not a realistic expectation. For one thing, the agencies were loathe to approve a direct intrusion upon the adoptee without first securing the parents' permission. It was reasoned that the seeking out of the adoptee without the intervening procedures would constitute a violation of the agreement made between the agencies and the parents. At the time of the consummation of these adoptions it had been understood that the agencies would withdraw from the family's life. There was an additional source of apprehension: there was no certainty that the adoptee had been informed by his parents that he was adopted. Neither was there any sureness that he was sufficiently stable emotionally to participate in a research interview that was seen as having potential for creating stress."

The authors go on, "The wisdom of the decision not to seek out the adopted child without the parents' prior approval was subsequently validated in the field operations. We were told in interviews with four sets of parents that they had never informed their children of their adoptive status. We also encountered a number of situations in which we felt that the adoptee's current adjustment was obviously too precarious to expose him to the research procedure."

I do not mean to put down this study. On the contrary, it offers interesting findings on the adjustment to adoption from the adoptive parents' point of view, and ought to be read by those who work in the field of adoption as well as by those who contemplate the adoption of a child. But if the "they" of the title is to be read as "the children," readers remain in the dark as to whether adoption has been a successful experience for them or not. Indeed, readers are told that, among the adopted adults, there were some for whom interviews on the subject were capable of "creating stress." Why? What was there about the experience that still could not be faced up to? There were adults whose parents believed they knew nothing of their adoption. One wonders: Did the adoptees suspect? Had they heard from outside sources? Were they ignorant of their origins or simply maintaining a tactful silence?

Pauline Albertson, a woman in her middle years who was adopted in infancy, seems typical of the many adults I interviewed in that she led a happy life and never quested for information on her biologic background nor voiced any desire to learn anything about the female who gave birth to her.

"It's not that I have no curiosity about my heritage," she said in response to my questions. "Of course there are times when I wonder what my mother looked like, the kind of woman she was . . . and, especially since I've had my own children, if she ever wonders what became of me. . . . But I'm quite secure about who I am as a person. More importantly, I know that such questions would cause pain to my adoptive parents, who are in every sense my real parents, the only ones I've known. I wouldn't hurt them for anything in the world." It follows that Pauline did not want me to use her real name.

Notes from an interview with Margaret, an attractive, literate, adoptive mother of three children, two now attending college at large state universities in the Midwest, the third a high school cheerleader.

Author: Do your children know they're adopted?

Margaret: Of course. We've never made a secret of it.

Author: Have you any information on their biologic parents?

Margaret: No. I never wanted any. The past doesn't matter in our lives. They're *my* children, and that's all any of us needs to know.

Author: Have any of the three children ever asked you anything about their biologic parents—where they came from, their ages, the circumstances behind their giving the infants up for adoption, any questions at all?

Mother: (vehemently) I should say not. And I would be very hurt if they did.

The adopted child who never asked, the adoptive parent who never heard the doubts expressed—neither can stand as proof that the adoptive situation works without qualification. Both have learned to carry on the business of living with one door of communication forever closed between them.

Many "adoptive experts" have written on this topic. Their findings deserve a wider audience than the professionals who most often are familiar with such studies. In a 1959 report entitled "Rear View Mirror: An Experience With Completed Adoptions," which was published in *The Social Worker*, Eleanor Lemon wrote:

> The sharing of experience by the [adult adoptee] persons interviewed has allowed us insight into the need of the adopted child to reconcile his identification with two sets of parents. It has supported the conviction that it is not enough for adoptive parents to share only the fact of adoption with the child, and to be vague and evasive about original parents. Curiosity, repressed or overt, and fantasy on the part of the child is a certain outcome—with all that this can mean

in interference with the richness of the emotional bond with adoptive parents. Such interference with the free-flowing relationships between parents and child means inevitably some degree of damage to the child's emotional development.

Later, writing on *Adopting Older Children,* child welfare specialist Alfred Kadushin addressed himself to the fantasy:

Theoretically, one of the principal conflicts for the child in adoption lies in the fact that he has, in reality, two sets of parents. The child who has never known a change in parentage splits the image of his parents into the two components to match the normal ambivalence felt for parents, the image of the good parent—congruent with positive ambivalence—who is the source of gratification, pleasure, rewards, and so forth, and the bad parent—congruent with the negative component of his ambivalence—who punishes, disciplines, frustrates, and denies the child. However, since the same parent both gratifies and punishes, the child is forced to resolve the fantasy and accept both the attractive and hateful aspects of the same parent figure. It is said that the adoptive child can invest each of his sets of parents with a different aspect of his ambivalence. As a result, the absent parent can be idealized.

Since the absent parent never punishes or disciplines, it is easy to see him as all loving, all gratifying. . . .

Whether the child of adoption seeks the fantasy parent or simply wants to know more about "Who am I?" the adoption world today must recognize a movement by adult adoptees that seeks to break open the seals on adoption records and to make available to responsible adults information on their past histories. There are many who argue that the denial of such information to those who are of age is a basic denial of their legal rights.

While laws differ from state to state, and are often more

flexible within certain agencies than others, the general procedure in adoption is to seal the records of the child as soon as an adoption is legalized, no matter what the age of the youngster being adopted. A new birth certificate is issued, with the correct date and city of birth. In the space provided for the names of the child's mother and father, the names of the adoptive parents are entered. All other history—names and ages of the original parents, grandparents where known, pertinent medical data—is relegated to locked files, not to be opened except under special conditions and by court order, which is extremely difficult to obtain.

The drama of this finality is touchingly described in Bard Lindeman's nonfiction account of *The Twins Who Found Each Other*, brothers who were separated at birth in Binghamton, New York, 1938, and who became Roger Brooks of Miami and Anthony Milasi of Binghamton. At some point, Anthony learned that he had a brother and went on a quest to locate his twin. His adoptive parents were unable to help him, for they did not know what had become of the boy, or even whether he was still alive. Over the years, Tony sought his brother. One day, "Tony drove home to Binghamton and went directly downtown to the Bureau of Vital Statistics. As he mounted the wooden porch steps that led to the Bureau offices he told himself he was finally going to find answers to his questions about his twin, for he knew his adoption papers were on file in this building. . . . As . . . the registrar listened to his story, she thought, 'Suppose one of my two boys was looking for his brother? Oh, God, I hope someone would help him!' Yet, there was nothing that she could do for Tony Milasi. She explained that under the law his adoption file was sealed and could only be opened, even to him, by a court order from a justice of the state supreme court." The brothers did eventually find one another, as stated in the book's title, based on a stranger's mistaking one for the other. They were identical twins.

Florence Fisher, an adoptee, was an adult who knew she was not a twin, but she spent twenty-one years of her life seeking to find out "Who do I look like?" As she tells her story, "I was seven years old when I came upon a photostat of an official-looking document hidden in a drawer of my parents' dresser. It had the word 'adopted' on it, an unfamiliar woman's name, and the names of the two people I'd always believed were my parents. Somehow, at that early age, it seemed to make sense to me. I knew I was adopted. I confronted my parents, who denied it at first, but who made certain to destroy the paper."

Years later, when her adoptive mother died, Florence Fisher found that the relatives who came to mourn talked about dividing the dead woman's possessions as if she, the daughter, didn't exist. "I didn't have a particularly happy adoptive experience nor was it bitterly unhappy," Florence recalls. "Although my material needs were taken care of, I couldn't communicate with the people who raised me. I do have an adoptive uncle who is like a father to me, and who is a most important person in my life. But I feel that the degree of happiness one finds in an adoptive home has no bearing on whether that person will suffer an identity crisis. It's an individual thing. Those adoptees who don't want to find anything out about their backgrounds are the lucky ones. What most people fail to understand is that the ones who do embark on a search are more interested in learning of their identity than they are in locating a second set of parents." Her story goes on:

Florence managed to obtain a copy of her amended birth certificate, which at least provided the name of the city of birth. There were many disappointments as leads led to dead ends. "Have you ever experienced being mistaken for another person?" Florence asks. "Well, whenever anyone would greet me with recognition and then, realizing his error, say, 'I'm sorry. You look like someone I know,' I'd grab his arm and demand, 'Who? Who do I look like?' Perhaps I had a sister somewhere . . . maybe the man or woman knew my mother. . . . Someplace in this world there had to be someone who looked like me." (Far-fetched? But it was just such recognition that led to the reunion of Roger Brooks and Anthony Milasi.)

At one point, Florence's search led to the office of the lawyer who arranged her adoption. He would not see her. When she badgered her childhood doctor for facts, he retorted, "You're illegitimate. Is that what you wanted to find out?" Over the years, Florence developed a routine of telephoning the hospital in which she was born, hoping that someday she would reach some clerk who, unwittingly, would provide her with the information she was seeking. The call that proved successful was one in which Florence pretended that she was about to leave on a trip, was in a terrible hurry, and required some information that was contained in the hospital's files: the name and address of her mother as listed on the certificate of birth. It was a ploy that Florence had used before. But this time—"Just a moment, please," said the youthful voice at the other end of the line. Pause. "Ah, here it is." And she went on to be more helpful than she could possibly imagine, making available that small bit of information it had taken Florence two decades to unearth.

How do you get in touch with a woman who has never seen you in her life—and who may never want to see you?

Florence now worried over that problem for a while. Finally, she traveled to the city in which her mother made her home and telephoned the lady, claiming that she was a distant relative who had only a short time to spend in her city. Could they get together? Her mother invited Florence to her home—which Florence could not agree to; she didn't want to invade the woman's privacy by announcing herself to the entire family. After she'd learned the name of her mother, Florence had done some investigation and found that the woman was married and the mother of two grown children. How do you enter their lives?

At Florence's suggestion, the two women met at her mother's place of business. "I didn't have to tell her who I was," recalls Florence. "She knew. *I look like her!*"

In subsequent visits, Florence's mother told her that she had been seventeen when she became pregnant, and had in fact married Florence's father in a brief ceremony, shot-gun variety, after which he had been encouraged to leave for points distant by the mother's parents—Florence's grandparents—who disapproved of the match. The couple accepted their daughter back home, with the condition that she surrender the child. Florence's mother did so, and subsequently made a new life for herself.

More recently, Florence located her father. Over the years, he had made several marriages, all of them childless. This was, then, a romantic turn for his life to take—to have his only child re-enter it. Of course, he was delighted to see her. A warm relationship followed easily. "Now," Florence says, "I know who I am, and I can pass my heritage on to my son and, someday, to my grandchildren."

To help others with similar yearnings, and to fight against the secrecy that surrounds the background of the adoptee, Florence Fisher and eleven adult adoptees founded the Adoptees Liberty Movement Association (ALMA, the Spanish word for "soul"). There now are more than one thousand members, some of them parents of adopted children who want to help these youngsters as they go through their individual crises of identity. Adoptees who consult ALMA are cautioned that reunion with biologic parents may not prove a happy experience. (Incidentally, the organization dislikes the term "biologic parent." "Each child has *natural* parents," says

Florence Fisher. "Many adoptive parents want to believe this isn't so.") One woman member who located her original mother was abusively, totally rejected by the woman. "It was worth it," she believes. "I then had to go home and rethink who I was, without the fantasy. I'm better off for it."

ALMA will not take on the work of "the search" for any of the people who come to the organization. Members are supportive to the person involved in the frustrating, often agonizing venture, but they do believe that the procedure is something the adoptee has to go through himself. To simplify this task, however, ALMA has embarked on a legal fight against sealed records as denying the basic rights of an adult individual to learn facts about himself. "How dare they say to me," asks Florence, "that if I want to see my own records I must show just cause?"

Whose right is paramount: the child's or that of the mother who surrendered that child in good faith that her privacy would be respected, and that she could go on to rebuild her life? To Florence Fisher, the answer is clear: "The child was never consulted when his future was decided. His right to know who he is comes first, with the proviso that tact be used if and when any contact is made."

"In the majority of cases, you do not upset a life," in the opinion of Jean Paton, a twice-adopted woman (her first adopted father died when she was two years old) who, since 1953, has been studying adoption from the viewpoint of the adult adoptee. She explains, "Adopted people are very sensitive to the situation their natural mother may be in."

Now retired from her lifetime career in social work where she was active in the fields of boarding-home children, surrender of children for adoption, and permanent foster care, Miss Paton directs Orphan Voyage, "a program of mutual aid and guidance for social orphans," from her home in Cedaredge, Colorado. What is a social orphan? According to Miss Paton's literature (she has written books and pamphlets on the subject), "A social orphan is a person whose loss of one or both parents has come about by a social decision, or whose parent loss, though natural or private in origin, has been reinforced by the attitudes and actions of society. Therefore, there are sources of social orphanhood other than illegitimacy, as: divorce, imprisonment, or simple absence."

In a unique service to its members, Orphan Voyage maintains a "reunion file," which matches registrations from adult adopted people and natural parents. Registration also is used by brothers and sisters who have been separated and who seek to find one another. Even before the establishment of ALMA, Orphan Voyage took the position that "the sealing of birth records is a violation of the basic rights of those whom it affects, that it fails to consider alternatives, and that it discourages the creative process of reconciliation." With his records sealed, the adult adoptee is left in the dark as to what his origins are and what hereditary traits he may be passing on to his children. In one case that came to my attention, a man who was adopted in infancy was being divorced by his wife because of his refusal to father children unless he came to know something of his medical history. Jean Paton has found that sealing the records gives the adopted person the fear that there is a stigma attached to his birth, perhaps something even worse than the illegitimate birth of which most adopted children are aware.

Until recently, most agency workers defended their pro-secrecy position by offering as proof the fact that they didn't have adopted people coming back to see their records. Jean Paton's response to this has been, "For many years, adopted people have had the idea that the answer to their request to see their files will be no, so they haven't gone."

Yet even today, a good number of adoption agencies remain rigid against revelation. Appearing on a recent television show, Natalie K. Evan, psychologist with New York's Spence Chapin agency, restated her (and the agency's) position clearly: "The cornerstone of adoption is confidentiality for *all* of the participants."

At the same time, and in the same city, evidence exists that the cornerstone may be nudged a bit without causing the entire building to topple. At the New York Foundling Hospital, Sister Bernard Marie, who is in charge of the home's closed records department, makes a policy of releasing information to adults—in some cases, to teenagers—who come back seeking to know of their backgrounds. That many *do* come back gives the lie to the argument that children of adoption, in the main, are content to live without knowledge of their past.

A genial, gray-haired septuagenarian who has spent more than a third of her life in adoption work, Sister Bernard Marie receives three or four letters a day from adoptees who want to learn more about themselves. Often, the search for identity comes disguised in other forms. "I receive letters from sixty year olds who claim they need this or that bit of information for purposes of social security," the sister reports. "At this time their adoptive parents are no longer living and these people finally have summoned up the nerve to ask questions about their background without fear of hurting anyone. Then there are the people who don't discover, until middle age, that they were adopted as infants. They want to know whatever facts are available. But my most frequent letter is one written by a young woman just before she is herself about to be married. She wants to know about her past as she plans for her future. Also, she's particularly interested in her medical history when she contemplates having a family of her own."

While Sister Bernard Marie will rarely go so far as to

contact the biologic mother (in some cases, she has done so—asking the woman if she would be willing to meet with the child to whom she gave birth), she has found that most adoptees are content with much less. "Little facts are precious. The first name of the biologic mother often is a treasure . . . or information on what the biologic father did to earn his living. One teen-ager who had a raucous voice—you could hear her from down the street when you were inside the house—was amazed to discover that our records indicated her mother was a gentle person, with a very soft voice. A short fellow who thought himself misplaced in a tall adoptive family felt less uncomfortable when told his original mother was five feet seven inches and his father more than six feet tall. You see, we had carefully matched our babies then, and he belonged in a tall family. This knowledge was important to that boy. It was all that he needed to know."

Acknowledgment of the child's heredity is extremely important, believes the sister, in giving the boy or girl regard for what he or she *brought into the adoptive home.* "Too many adoptive parents tend to make the child aware of what they have given him," she believes. "And it is true that, materially, the child generally has been placed upward. But some children then develop a feeling that the adoptive family is so much better, they can't possibly measure up. This is particularly true in the case of the child who is adopted at an advanced age. His use of inappropriate language or his sloppy table habits are likely to annoy the members of his new family. Correcting him, his adoptive parent may say, 'We don't do that in our home.' The child then feels as a stranger within that home. He will learn to conform to the norms, but he never will truly feel like one of the family."

Do the mothers of the children who were surrendered for adoption get in touch with the Foundling Hospital? "Yes," says Sister Bernard Marie, "but they aren't looking for a reunion with the child. Generally, they just want to know if we've kept in touch with the child and if he or she is well. They may have had to give the child up, but most of them can tell you, to the hour, the child's age at any given moment."

Michigan social worker Kay Donley of the Spaulding for Children agency conducted a discovery group of adult adoptees, and found: (a) that there was a continuing fantasy of a one-way glass through which grown children could view their biologic parents ("Who do I look like?") but not meet with them nor re-enter their lives; (b) they had greater interest in the presence of siblings than in the whereabouts of parents; (c) that curiosity expressed by the adoptees was a separate quality, and not linked to rejection of the adoptive parents.

Many adoptive parents are beginning to recognize this, too. A good number of those who favored secrecy when their adoptive children were very young (perhaps coupled with fear that the biologic parent would arrive on the scene and seek to reclaim the youngster) have come to adopt more liberal positions in regard to revelation as these same children approach adulthood. While most do not go so far as to advocate abolishment of the sealed record, many are beginning to take the position expressed by an active member of New York's Adoptive Parents Committee at a meeting held in 1972. Admitting that he had followed the practice of the past and refrained from asking any questions about his adoptive son's background at the time of adoption seventeen years earlier (on the theory that what you don't know won't hurt you), the gentleman now voiced his belief that this ignorance was in fact hurting his now teen-age son. "There are questions the boy lives with. Because I love him, I'd like to help him by providing some of the answers, but I can't," this father said.

He went on to advise parents involved in the process

of adoption today to gather as much information as is available on the child's background. "If you feel it will rock the boat at the agency and hinder your chances of adopting," he added in a telling aside, "wait until the adoption is finalized and then go back to the agency and *demand* the facts. Someday, they may prove important to your child."

Leah Marks, former staff attorney for New York's Citizens' Committee for Children and now deputy executive officer of the family court, views the denial of the right of an adopted child to get his or her family medical history as a major deficiency in children's rights. Whether the adult who was once the child of adoption must someday be granted the right to all of the facts that concern him— those bits of information that have been sealed away from his scrutiny for his lifetime—is a question that must engage members of the legal and social work professions now and in the immediate future.

Appendix

BIBLIOGRAPHY

BOOKS

A Dream Deferred: Child Welfare in New York City. New York: Citizens' Committee for Children of New York, Inc., 1971.

Anderson, David C. *Children of Special Value: Interracial Adoption in America.* New York: St. Martin's Press, 1971.

Buck, Pearl S. *Children for Adoption.* New York: Random House, 1965.

De Hartog, Jan. *The Children (A Personal Record for the Use of Adoptive Parents).* New York: Atheneum Press, 1968.

Fanshel, David and Shinn, Eugene B., *Dollars and Sense in Foster Care of Children: A Look at Cost Factors.* New York: Child Welfare League of America, 1972.

Festinger, Trudy. *Why Some Choose Not to Adopt Through Agencies.* New York: Metropolitan Applied Research Center, 1972.

Frontiers in Adoption: Finding Homes for the "Hard to Place." Ann Arbor, Mich.: 1969. Council on Adoptable Children.

Haitch, Richard. *Orphans of the Living: The Foster Care Crisis*. New York: Public Affairs Committee in co-operation with the Child Welfare League of America, 1968.

Herzog, Elizabeth, and others. *Families for Black Children: The Search for Adoptive Parents,* Parts I and II. A co-operative report of the Children's Bureau, Office of Child Development, U. S. Department of Health, Education and Welfare, and the Social Research Group, George Washington University. Washington, D.C.: U. S. Government Printing Office, 1971.

International Adoption Handbook One. Minneapolis, Minn.: OURS, 1972.

Isaac, Rael Jean, with Joseph Spencer, legal consultant. *Adopting a Child Today*. New York: Harper & Row, 1965.

Jaffee, Benson and Fanshel, David. *How They Fared in Adoption: A Follow-up Study*. New York and London: Columbia University Press, 1970.

Kadushin, Alfred. *Adopting Older Children*. New York: Columbia University Press, 1970.

Kim, Hi Taik and Reid, Elaine. *After a Long Journey* (a study on the process of initial adjustment of the half and full Korean children adopted by American families . . .). Minneapolis, Minn.: University of Minnesota School of Social Work, 1970.

Kirk, H. David. *Shared Fate: A Theory of Adoption and Mental Health*. New York: The Free Press of Glencoe, 1964.

Lindeman, Bard. *The Twins Who Found Each Other*. New York: William Morrow & Co., 1969.

ARTICLES

Branham, Ethel. "One Parent Adoptions," *Children*, May–June 1970, Vol. 17, No. 3.

Brooten, Gary. "The Multiracial Family," New York *Times Magazine*, September 26, 1971.

Dunne, Phyllis. "Placing Children of Minority Groups for Adoption," *Children*, March–April 1958, Vol. 5, No. 2.

Gallagher, Ursula M. "The Adoption of Mentally Retarded Children," *Children,* January–February 1968, Vol. 15, No. 1.

Hornecker, Alice. "Adoption Opportunities for the Handicapped," *Children,* July–August 1962, Vol. 9, No. 4.

Kadushin, Alfred. "Reversibility of Trauma: A Follow-up Study of Children Adopted When Older," *Social Work,* October 1967, Vol. 12, No. 4.

—— and Seidl, Frederick W. "Adoption Failure: A Social Work Postmortem," *Social Work,* July 1971, Vol. 16.

Lemon, Eleanor. "Rear View Mirror: An Experience With Completed Adoptions," *The Social Worker,* June–July 1959, Vol. 27.

Miller, Helen. "Recent Developments in Korean Services for Children," *Children,* January–February 1971, Vol. 18, No. 1.

Morgenstern, Joseph. "The New Face of Adoption," *Newsweek,* September 13, 1971.

Skeels, Harold M. "Effects of Adoption on Children From Institutions," *Children,* January–February 1965, Vol. 12, No. 1.

Thompson, Era Bell. "The Plight of Black Babies in South Vietnam," *Ebony,* December 1972.

LIST OF CITIZENS ORGANIZATIONS
CONCERNED WITH ADOPTION

This section has been included to aid persons interested in obtaining information on adoption news at the local level. It is also hoped that citizens in the separate states might here locate a chapter of a group with which they could affiliate. Officers and addresses may change from time to time. Periodically, new associations are formed. A query addressed to any of the organizations listed should, at the least, elicit such information.

Alabama

Adoptive Parents Association
of Alabama
P. O. Box 5166
Huntsville, Alabama 35805

Arizona

Arizona Families for Children
% Mrs. Richard L. Keefe
P. O. Box 17951
Tucson, Arizona 85710

The Open Door Society of
Phoenix
% Mrs. Madeline Gluck
8332 East Rose Lane
Scottsdale, Arizona 85253

California

Adopted Parents Association
% Roy Hartman, President
813 University Avenue
Burbank, California 91504

Chow, Inc.
% Robert McGown, President
3712 Chamberlain Way
Carmichael, California 95608

WINGS
% Mrs. Mabel Fouse, President
1528 South Mayo Street
Compton, California 90221

Orange County Adoptive Parents' Association
P. O. Box 1314
Huntington Beach, California 92647

Parents' Adoption League
120 East Ocean Boulevard
Long Beach, California 90802

Open Door Society of Los Angeles
% Ruth Campbell
3848 Mt. Vernon Drive
Los Angeles, California 90008

Open Door Society of Los Angeles
% Mr. and Mrs. Truman Clark
1054 West 78th Street
Los Angeles, California 90044

Adoptive Parents Association
P. O. Box 66373
Los Angeles, California 90006

Humboldt County Council on Adoptable Children (COAC)
1371 Whitmire Street
McKinleyville, California 95521

Adoptive Family Association
P. O. Box 1236
Ontario, California 91762

Adoptaides
Panorama Towers
8155 Van Nuys Boulevard
Panorama City, California 91402

Open Door Society of San Bernardino and Riverside Counties
% Mrs. Linda Dunne
250 East Blaine
Riverside, California 92507

Friends of Foster Children
% 1. Appaloosa
Rolling Hills, California 94103

The Carriage Trade
1680 Mission Street
San Francisco, California 94103

Families Adopting Interracially (FAIR)
% Mrs. Jim Thornton
5147 Forest View Drive
San Jose, California 95129

Adoptive Parent Organization
1062 Grape Street
Sunnyvale, California 94087

Vista Del Mar Adoption Guild
% Sue Stutz
5469 Katherine Avenue
Van Nuys, California 91401

Adopted Children's Association of Whittier, Inc.
P. O. Box 797
Whittier, California 94508

Colorado

Fortunate Few Mothers' Club
% Ms. Barbara Darling, President
8363 Sheridan Court
Arvada, Colorado 80003

North Area Mothers' Club
% Mrs. Judy Martine, President
6238 Ingalls Street
Arvada, Colorado 80002

Parents for All Children
% Mr. and Mrs. Bob Sample, Co-Chairmen
875 Alpine, Apt. #5
Boulder, Colorado 80302

Colorado Adoptive Parents Association
% Mrs. Sam Dalton
1331 West Evans
Denver, Colorado 80223

Lucky Mothers' Club
% Mrs. Joyce Gregory, President
1712 S. Pontiac
Denver, Colorado 80222

Parents for All Children
% Mrs. Skip Foseter
355 Balsam
Denver, Colorado 80226

Foothills Mothers' Club
% Mrs. Sandra True, President
120 Flower
Lakewood, Colorado 80026

South Suburban Mothers' Club
% Mrs. Art Metting, President
4541 South Utica
Littleton, Colorado 80120

Connecticut

Open Door Society of Connecticut, Inc.
P. O. Box 2162
Meriden, Connecticut 06450

Delaware

Friday's Child
% Mrs. Frank Czeiner
8 Chadd Road
Newark, Delaware 19711

District of Columbia

D. C. Metropolitan Area
   Council on Adoptive
   Children
% Mrs. Judy Pope
622 C Street S.E.
Washington, D.C. 20003

Florida

WE KARE
% Mr. and Mrs. William
   Clark
200 Grace Boulevard
Altamonte Springs, Florida
   32701

Susannah K. Becker (an informal group)
1209 Obispo
Coral Gables, Florida 33824

Council on Adoptable Chil-
   dren
P. O. Box 721
Miami, Florida 33145

Georgia

CSRA Adoptive Parents Or-
   ganization
% Mrs. Mogan Wheeler
1652 Pendleton Road
Augusta, Georgia 30904

CSRA Parents Organization
% Francis S. Welp, SSG, U. S.
   Army
1952-A Story Drive
Fort Gordon, Georgia 30905

Illinois

Open Door Society of Illinois,
   Inc.
Chapters:
514 Hackberry Drive
Arlington Heights, Illinois
   60004

% Mr. Rol Jeske
639 Elsinoor Lane
Crystal Lake, Illinois 60014

% Mrs. Christine Roos
4850 Lake Park Avenue
Chicago, Illinois 60615

% Mr. Jack Kerrill, President
720 Madison Street
Evanston, Illinois 60202

% Mr. and Mrs. Jeff Strack
R.R. #2
Sycamore, Illinois 60178

Council on Adoptable Chil-
   dren of Illinois
Chapters:
Quad City Council
810 54th Street
Moline, Illinois 61265

1002 S. Busey
Urbana, Illinois 61801

Chosen Parents of Illinois
% Mr. and Mrs. Herman H.
   Harden
P. O. Box 7
Raritan, Illinois 61471

Mr. Wes Thompson
1420 West Clarewood Court
Peoria, Illinois 61614

OURS
Gerry and Judy Stanley
1404 Berwin Street
Spring Grove, Illinois 60081

Indiana

Association for the Rights of
Children (ARC)
Chapters:
4323 South Park Drive
Fort Wayne, Indiana 46806

% Ms. Bonnie Buescher
4033 North Euclid Avenue
Indianapolis, Indiana 46226

25 West 49th Street
Indianapolis, Indiana 46208

R. 4 Box 813
Kokomo, Indiana 46901

% Mrs. Thomas A. Magers
606 North Scott Street
South Bend, Indiana 46616

Open Door Society
% Mr. and Mrs. Daniel Boy-
lan
3934 Fairfield Avenue
Fort Wayne, Indiana 46807

Council on Adoptable Children
% Mrs. Moses W. Gray
1929 Copenhaver Drive
Indianapolis, Indiana 46208

The Open Door
P. O. Box 2092
South Bend, Indiana 46615

Iowa

HOLTAP of Iowa
% Mr. Warren Cateron
3220 East Douglas
Des Moines, Iowa 50317

Council on Adoptable Children
411 West Clonton
Indianola, Iowa 50125

Open Door Society
% Mr. Jerry Musser
R. R. #4
Iowa City, Iowa 52240

OURS
Chapters:
% Jack and Sharon Ellis
616 Sunrise Circle
Muscatine, Iowa 52761

% Calvin and Esther Pooler
3035 Clark Street
P. O. Box 172
Charles City, Iowa 50616

Sharing Thru Adoption
% Mr. David Alfredson
5418 6th Avenue
Sioux City, Iowa 51106

Kansas

National Council of Adoptive
 Parents Organization
 (NCAPO)
% Rev. Gilbert P. Herrman
Catholic Social Service
2546 20th Street
Great Bend, Kansas 67530

Kansas American Koreans,
 Inc.
% Mr. Larry Sanders
2602 North Monroe
Hutchinson, Kansas 67501

Families of Adopted Mixed-
 Race Children
% Mrs. John Boulton, Presi-
 dent
1721 Kentucky
Lawrence, Kansas 66044

Adoptive Mothers' Club
% Mrs. Nancee Price, Secretary
1206 High
Topeka, Kansas 66604

Maine

Families for Adoptable Chil-
 dren
Box 416
North Windham, Maine 04062

Maryland

Open Door Society of Mary-
 land
P. O. Box 856
Columbia, Maryland 21044

Think Adoption (TAD)
5891 Morningbird Lane
Columbia, Maryland 21045

National Council of Adoptive
 Parents Organization
% Mr. Morton Friedman
9140 Good Luck Road
Lanham, Maryland 20801

Council on Adoptable Children
% Farley
10513 Bucknell Place
Wheaton, Maryland 20902

Massachusetts

The Open Door Society of
 Massachusetts, Inc.
600 Washington Street
Boston, Massachusetts 02111

Michigan

Adoptive Family Association
 of Western Michigan
% Roger Johnson
545 Gladstone, S.E.
Grand Rapids, Michigan
 49506

Grand Rapids Mothers of
 Korean Orphans
% Mrs. Claude Van Ooyen
3710 Cheyenne Drive
Grandville, Michigan 49418

Muskegon Mothers' Group
% Mr. and Mrs. Henry De-
 Jong
1863 Amity Street
Muskegon, Michigan 49442

Beachcombers
% Mrs. Raymond Brower
526 James Street
Spring Lake, Michigan 49456

OURS
Chapters:
% Larry and Donna Eggberts
2970 West F Avenue
Kalamazoo, Michigan 49007

% Richard and Shirley Minarik
Route 1
Shelbyville, Michigan 49344

Council on Adoptable Children in Michigan
Chapters:
% Mrs. Peter Forsythe
1205 Olivia
Ann Arbor, Michigan 48104

% Mrs. Joyce Maisel
19478 Prest
Detroit, Michigan 49235

% Mrs. Ronald P. Titsworth
2737 Golfside Lane
Flint, Michigan 48504

% Mrs. John Hoffman
1028 Hoffman Street
Petoskey, Michigan 49770

1012 Oak Street
Kalamazoo, Michigan 49008

% Ms. Barbara Parson
2125 Clearview Road
Lansing, Michigan 48917

20036 15 Mile Road
Mt. Clemens, Michigan 48043

% Mr. and Mrs. James Hawley
830 Airport Road
Muskegon, Michigan 49441

Minnesota

OURS
Headquarters:
3148 Humboldt Avenue South
Minneapolis, Minnesota 55408
(Branches throughout Minnesota)

Open Door Society of Minnesota
3801 Independence Avenue
Minneapolis, Minnesota 55427

Associated Parents
% Childrens' Home Society
2230 Como Avenue
St. Paul, Minnesota 55108

Missouri

Missouri Open Door Society
Chapters:
6119 Waterman
St. Louis, Missouri 63112

P. O. Box 1856
Bois D'Arc, Missouri 65612

814 Bluff Street
Fulton, Missouri 65251

P. O. Box 7087
Kansas City, Missouri 64113

222 East Lafayette
Palmyra, Missouri 63461

304 Jones Avenue
Warrensburg, Missouri 64093

The Adoptive Mothers' Club
% Mrs. Raymond Eifert
P. O. Box 382
Illmo, Missouri 63754

Nebraska

Nebraska Adoptive Parents
  Club
% Mrs. Anne Coyne
1130 West 79th Street
Lincoln, Nebraska 68505

New Hampshire

Frontiers in Adoption
% Mrs. David Carter
R.F.D. #4
Concord, New Hampshire
  03301

Planned Parenthood Association of Uppervalley
14 Parkhurst Street
Lebanon, New Hampshire
  03766

New Jersey

Southern New Jersey Adoptive Parents Organization
% Mrs. Rosemary Wells
614 South Drive
Atlantic City, New Jersey
  08401

Adoptive Mothers' Club of
  Morris County
% Mrs. Carole Walters
114 Flanders Netcong Road
Flanders, New Jersey 07836

Adoptive Parents' League of
  New Jersey, Inc.
15 Inglewood Lane
Matawan, New Jersey 07747

Mrs. Allan W. Vliet
18 Altamont Court
Morristown, New Jersey
  07960

Frontiers in Adoption
163 Nassau Street
Princeton, New Jersey 08540

South Jersey Adoption Association
P. O. Box 583
Pleasantville, New Jersey
  08232

National Council of Adoptive
  Parents Organization
P. O. Box 543
Teaneck, New Jersey 07666

Council on Adoptable Children
617 Boulevard
Westfield, New Jersey 07090

HOLTAP of New Jersey
P. O. Box 234 Old Highway
Whitehouse, New Jersey
  08888

Concerned Parents for Adoption
% Mrs. Julie Brohan, President
200 Parsippany Road
Whippany, New Jersey 07981

New York

Adoptive Parents Committee
Box 93
East Northport, New York 11731

Adoptive Families of Westchester
P. O. Box 127
Dobbs Ferry, New York 10522

Open Door Society of Greater New York
% Mrs. Faye Caperna
12 Library Lane
Holbrook, New York 11741

Adoptive Parents Committee of Utica
% Mr. Michael Palmiero
New Hartford, New York 13413

Adoptive Parents Committee, Inc.
210 Fifth Avenue
New York, New York 10010

New York Council on Adoptable Children
61 Gramercy Park North
New York, New York 10003

Council of Adoptive Parents
67 Wood Haven Drive
Rochester, New York 14625

Open Door Society of Long Island
% Ms. Shirley Damboise
22 Yerk Avenue
Ronkonkoma, New York 11779

Families for the Future
2 Ellsworth Avenue
Scotia, New York 12302

Families for Inter-Racial Adoption
100 DeWitt Road
Syracuse, New York 13214

Parents for All Children of Chautauqua County
25 Chestnut Street
Westfield, New York 14787

Parents for All Children of Western New York
% Mrs. Sandra Isaacs
65 Fancher Avenue
Buffalo, New York 14223

North Carolina

Council on Adoptable Children
% Mr. R. Gwyn
Chapel Hill, North Carolina 27514

Ohio

Adopt a Child Today (ACT)
Chapters:
P. O. Box 20010
Cleveland, Ohio 44120

% Michael Freedman
4680 Edon Road
Kent, Ohio 44240

% Richard Chartoff
1020 Brayton Avenue
Cincinnati, Ohio 45215

% Dennis M. Gaughn
P. O. Box 20010
Cleveland, Ohio 44120

% Tim Nyros
200 East Oakland Avenue
Columbus, Ohio 43201

% George Edgington
561 North Fairfield Road
Dayton, Ohio 45430

Open Door Society of Cincinnati
3809 Ault Park Avenue
Cincinnati, Ohio 45208

Council on Adoptable Chil-
dren
Chapters:
% Mr. Ed Degenhardt
26580 Mallard Avenue
Euclid, Ohio 44132

146 Hannum Avenue
Rossford, Ohio 43460

The Adoptive Parents Club
% Mrs. Patricia Maulorico,
President
1020 Dawnwood Drive
Parma, Ohio 44134

Oregon

Open Door for Adoptable
Children
% Mrs. Kathy Nordahl
4875 Garnet Street
Eugene, Oregon 97405

MOKY
% Mrs. K. Cutler, President
147 Roundup Drive
Eugene, Oregon 97401

PLAN
842 Southwest Government
Street
Newport, Oregon 97365

Open House Association
% Mrs. Lloyd Meskimen
4054 North Colonial
Portland, Oregon 97227

Portland Open Door Society
% Mrs. Bob Riddle
1736 South East 143rd Street
Portland, Oregon 97233

Pennsylvania

P.O.A.
% Mr. Kenneth Westgate
1426 Walnut Street
Allentown, Pennsylvania
18102

Council on Adoptable Children
Chapters:
P. O. Box 3461
Erie, Pennsylvania 16512

P. O. Box 14
Gwynedd, Pennsylvania
19436

Adoptive Parents Group
(APG)
% Dr. Dennis Lebofsky
14021 Farady Street
Philadelphia, Pennsylvania
19116

Welcome House Adoptive
Parents Group
% Mrs. Alberta Cohen
R. D. #4, Box 152A
Quakertown, Pennsylvania
18951

Parents of Adopted Children
122 West Springettsburg Avenue
York, Pennsylvania 17403

Rhode Island

Rhode Island Families for Interracial Adoption
433 Elmwood Avenue
Providence, Rhode Island
02907

South Dakota

Council on Adoptable Children
% Mr. and Mrs. Ken Knutson
Box 168
Colman, South Dakota 57017

Tennessee

Council on Adoptable Children of Tennessee
% Mr. M. Mihal
224 Woodmont
Nashville, Tennessee 37205

Texas

Adopted Families of Texas
704 Beta Circle
Pasadena, Texas 77503

Council on Adoptable Children of Texas
P. O. Box 33303
Houston, Texas 77033

Vermont

Room for One More
Chapters:
% Mrs. Nancy Van Gulden
Williston, Vermont 05495

% Mrs. Alfred Fenton
Box 115
Wallingford, Vermont 05773

Virginia

Friends of the Children's
Home Society of Virginia
% Mrs. J. R. Williams, President
311 Clovelly Road
Richmond, Virginia 23221

Washington

Adoptive Family Association
30463 4th Avenue
Federal Way, Washington
98002

Open Door Society
312 North Sherman
Olympia, Washington 98501

Concerned Parents for Children
725 West 6th
Port Angeles, Washington
98362

Focus on Adoption Committee
% Mrs. Marcia W. Baldwin
3337 Hunter Boulevard S.
Seattle, Washington 98144

Interracial Family Association
% Mrs. Patricia Ford
3332 Hunter Boulevard South
Seattle, Washington 98144

Washington Association of
Christian Adoptive Parents
4424 Francis North
Seattle, Washington 98103

Wisconsin

Open Door Society
1128 Mitscher Avenue
Eau Claire, Wisconsin 54701

Open Door Society
Chapters:
% Mrs. Ralph Carus
3623 South 23rd Street
Milwaukee, Wisconsin 53221

% Mr. Marvin Winter, President
712 Marshall Avenue
Milwaukee, Wisconsin 53172

% Mrs. Reno Kuehnel
Rt. ⌗1, Box 283
Newton, Wisconsin 53063

Adoptive Insights
306 North West Avenue
Waukesha, Wisconsin 53186

Canada

The Open Door Society, Inc.
Chapters:
1370 Bank Street
Ottawa, Ontario, Canada

% LaSpadete
1060 Champigny
Duvernay, Laval
Quebec, Canada

5 Weredale Park
Montreal 215
Quebec, Canada

Families for Children
6 Salisbury Road
Pointe Claire 720
Quebec, Canada

Adopt Indian Metis
2240 Albert Street
Regina, Saskatchewan, Canada

Europe

Parent to Parent Information
on Adoption Services
26, Belsize Grove
London NW3, England

International Committee of
Adoptive Parents
% Dr. Giuseppe Cicorella,
President
Viale Brenta 7
20139 Milano, Italy

South Australia

Integration League of South
Australia (ILSA)
48 Green Street
St. Morris, South Australia

Australia

Adoptive Parents Association
% Ms. Angela Coffey
"Warralong"—Moorooduo
Road
Baxter, Victoria, Australia